BethRedman

SOULSISTER

Regal

From Gospel Light
Ventura, California, U.S.A.

PUBLISHED BY REGAL BOOKS
FROM GOSPEL LIGHT
VENTURA, CALIFORNIA, U.S.A.
Regal PRINTED IN THE U.S.A.

Regal Books is a ministry of Gospel Light, a Christian publisher dedicated to serving the local church. We believe God's vision for Gospel Light is to provide church leaders with biblical, user-friendly materials that will help them evangelize, disciple and minister to children, youth and families.

It is our prayer that this Regal book will help you discover biblical truth for your own life and help you meet the needs of others. May God richly bless you.

For a free catalog of resources from Regal Books/Gospel Light, please call your Christian supplier or contact us at 1-800-4-GOSPEL *or* www.regalbooks.com.

Originally published by Kingsway Communications, Ltd., Lottbridge Drove, Eastbourne BN23 6NT, England.

Edited by Amy Spence

Library of Congress Cataloging-in-Publication Data
Redman, Beth.
    Soul sister / Beth Redman.
        p. cm.
Includes bibliographical references.
    ISBN 0-8307-3212-8 (pbk.)
    1. Teenage girls—Religious life. 2. Teenage girls—Conduct of life.
I. Title.
    BV4551.3.R43 2004
    248.8'33—dc22   2003021965

1 2 3 4 5 6 7 8 9 10 11 12 13 14 15 / 10 09 08 07 06 05 04

Rights for publishing this book in other languages are contracted by Gospel Light Worldwide, the international nonprofit ministry of Gospel Light. Gospel Light Worldwide also provides publishing and technical assistance to international publishers dedicated to producing Sunday School and Vacation Bible School curricula and books in the languages of the world. For additional information, visit www.gospellightworldwide.org; write to Gospel Light Worldwide, P.O. Box 3875, Ventura, CA 93006; or send an e-mail to info@gospellightworldwide.org.

DEDICATION

For Anna Emilia DeFelippo—a true and faithful friend,
a constant encouragement and support, my beautiful
soul sister—I love you.

CONTENTS

INTROS FROM THE BOYS

In one way, I'm totally unqualified to write an introduction to this book for soul sisters. I do have a wife, a daughter and two younger sisters, but I'd still never dare to claim that I understand women!

On the other hand, my wife, Beth, is very well equipped to write on this subject. First, and most important, she has an inspiring passion for God. And second, she lives with a strong desire to see young women today grow in the truth and ways of God. Ever since I met Beth, she's been a listening ear to many young women and often offers godly and timely advice to those she meets. This said, I'm delighted that some of the same guidance now gets to make it into a book for many more young women to hear.

This world is tough for a young woman to grow up in. Life today seems to be crammed full of pressures, temptations and knockdowns for the average girl. I've witnessed some of the challenges for a soul sister today—in the lives of Beth, my sisters, Ellie and Sarah, and even more frighteningly, our little daughter. I've come across others who've been completely thrown off course by the pressures of today's image-consumed and soul-burdening society. In some ways it's a pretty bleak situation. Yet there is a truth that can set us free. In this book,

Beth takes soul sisters everywhere on a quest to pursue that beautiful truth—the incredible Word of God.

I am so proud of Beth for pouring her heart out in this way. There were many early mornings and late nights spent writing, as she faithfully juggled the balance of being a wife, a mother and an author. God has entrusted Beth with a fantastic gift to communicate the wisdom and passion He has placed in her heart. I pray she will inspire you in your walk with God as much as she has inspired me in mine.

Matt Redman

I've always found Beth to be honest, caring, passionate and great fun. There's never a dull moment with her. In this book, I find the exact same qualities. As I sat down to read it, I was intrigued to know what I'd learn about the ways of women. What I found was a down-to-earth, practical and honest book about living life as a girl for God. Here are words of wisdom and encouragement that help us face those tough issues that life throws at us.

Personally, I found it to be very helpful and inspiring. There's stuff in this book that all men should read. I remember when reading Beth's first book, which was similar in subject matter to this one, I felt the need to create some excuse about why I was reading it. I think I said it was for research purposes! Well, guys, if you need to, make up an excuse. Buy it for your sister and read it first. There are truths within this book that need to be heard and acted on. You can't read this book without being challenged. It provokes a response that can at times be uncomfortable, but it's necessary as we open ourselves to be changed more into Christ's likeness.

The thing I loved most about this book was that it left you in no doubt where the answers to life lie. This book is unashamedly about God—His heart for us, His love and mercy shown to us and His promises made to us. It is the truth of knowing God that will heal us and ultimately bring contentment and peace to our lives. After reading this book, I was left first and foremost thinking, *What an awesome and wonderful God we serve.*

Tim Hughes

This is a great book. Like its author, it is honest, funny and full of insight. Beth has been a close friend for a number of years. She is passionate in her pursuit of God. She has a love of the Bible that is infectious. She also is blessed with a frightening dose of what I can only describe as women's intuition. Sometimes I have wondered if she has my mind bugged. I'm sure she often knows what I'm feeling before I do!

This book is Beth all over. She tells it as it is. She can share with integrity, because she has known pain in her own life. Yet through the pain she has found God, His truth and His healing. Because Beth loves the Bible, she knows how much God's words can change lives. God's Word is all over this book, and that is why I am convinced it will set many girls free. While it is really important to know that people understand us, and while good advice is precious and counseling very helpful, in the end only the truth sets us free.

This book is so encouraging because it is packed with truth. In a world in which we are lied to and manipulated into believing things about ourselves that are destructive, this book will, I believe, be life changing for thousands of girls. Like its author, it is vulnerable and compassionate, inspiring and encouraging, and extremely practical, because it always points to the God who is the way, the truth and the life.

Mike Pilavachi

ACKNOWLEDGMENTS

First of all I want to thank my husband, Matt, who has always encouraged me, loved me and spurred me on. He willingly put his life on hold to support me while I was writing this book. Matt, there is no one else like you—Maisey, Noah and I are so blessed by your love and your true heart for God. Thank you—XXX.

Thanks to my two gorgeous babies for being patient and going with the flow while I was up in the attic writing for hours on end! Massive thanks and appreciation to Corin D'enno for Wednesdays and to Rachel and Jo at Elm House for the morning sessions!

Mike Pilavachi—once again you have supported me in writing this book and running with the vision of Soul Sister. I am so grateful that you are for me and behind me. You are my family and my faithful friend; and Matt and I love you very much!

Tim Hughes—our little brother—thanks for your encouragement and for your friendship. We are very proud of you.

Thanks to Bill Greig III, Bill Denzel and the Regal Books family for all your hard work and encouragement.

Don Williams—I am so grateful for your wisdom and your vast knowledge of the Bible. You put in many hours for me. Thanks.

Sarah Adams—thanks for going above and beyond your job description.

To Vicky Beeching and the girls on the Soul Sister board: Ali, Andreana, Rachel and Bee. Thank you for your support, your time and your vulnerability—you are faithful and beautiful girls of God.

Finally, to my two soul sisters-in-law—Ellie and Sarah. I love the way you have persevered and followed after God. You inspire me, and I thank God I am part of your family.

WELCOME TO THE TRUTH

Teenage magazine advice columns receive hundreds of letters every week. Desperate young girls ask huge questions about themselves, their struggles, their sexuality, their family and their pain: Why does this happen? What should I do? Who can I turn to? And so the faithful "agony aunts" dish out their advice, sometimes leaving an address or a phone number. Generally, though, that's the last you'll hear from them. They don't write or phone—you are on your own.

Fortunately, God has written the most incredible answers to our problem-page letters. If we choose to read them, we can expect to find direct answers in times of need and a personal message of love, grace, wisdom and affirmation. The Bible brings tender truth and powerful answers in times of pain and confusion. God has given us many amazing gifts—not only His Son, Jesus, and His Holy Spirit, but also His Word, the Bible, a book we can hold in our hands to hear straight from His heart and mind.

THE BIBLE IS OUR MANUAL FOR LIFE

As a teenage girl today it is so easy to lose the way. We are enter-tained by television and magazines, gossip and chatter. All of these things are distractions. They cause us to fill our days with everything but God, and the result is that many of us find ourselves living in an unsatisfied state.

Matt and I had just moved to a new area and were forever getting lost. Fortunately, we had use of a car with a built-in satellite navigation system. All we needed to do was type in where we wanted to go and the car spoke out directions till we reached our destination. This system was an amazing tool that stopped us from getting lost again!

That is just like the Bible. God has given us a book full of powerful wisdom and advice. It is not out-of-date or irrelevant; in fact, there is stuff in the Bible for every situation you may face as a young girl today. But where do you start and how do you find this truth?

If you were lost in London, you wouldn't just randomly open your guidebook and expect it to direct you. To use the guidebook effectively, you would find out where you needed to go and see what the book had to say about it. It is the same for the Bible. Although sometimes you can flip open a page and find an answer to a problem, it is more helpful to find out which particular chapter or verse contains the advice or help you need.

Later on in this book, we will take a look at which verses in the Bible to read when you are struggling in a particular situation. We'll also discuss how to actually make time to read it every day. Many of us race around in the morning trying on several different outfits, applying lip gloss and stuffing in a slice of toast and jam before quickly saying, "Oh, yes, and God please bless my day"—and that is our quiet time! We will face many things during that day—unfortunately not just success and laughter, but also possibly temptation, hurt, selfishness, disappointment and stress. We will need more than just a quick fix to get us through.

Several years ago I was in a horrible dilemma. Suddenly, I felt a strong tug to go to my room and pick up my Bible. I remember thinking out loud, "But what should I read?" I opened to the book of Romans, which I was reading through that week, and my eyes were drawn to a passage that nearly knocked me off my feet. It was as if God had written me a personal letter about my exact situation and what I should do about it. God had spoken directly to me through a book that was written nearly 2,000 years ago, and yet its words are powerful and true for today.

I became aware that I lived my life taking advice from everyone but God. I took my Bible with me occasionally to the meeting on a Sunday, or read through it just before I nodded off to sleep, but I had never really used it in the way it was meant. Psalm 119:105 says, "Your word is a lamp to my feet"—it brings light and life, clarity and power. From that day on I have not been able to look at the Bible in the same way.

Recently, just before our second baby was born, we found ourselves in a stressful dilemma. We had returned from a short stay in America and were preparing to relocate from Watford to the south. Unfortunately, our housing plans went a bit pear-shaped. The house we were going for fell through again and again. We ended up moving seven times, from one temporary place to another, not only confusing our toddler, but also causing us to feel unsettled and confused. Almost eight months into my pregnancy, we moved back to Watford, feeling worn out and disillusioned. Soon after that our baby son, Noah Luca, arrived. He was four weeks early and came out struggling for breath. The doctors moved him immediately to intensive care where he remained in critical condition for several days.

Many people gave us support and counsel, but the place we gained the most strength from was the Bible. One verse I read in Joshua said, "I will never leave you nor forsake you" (1:5). I knew that God was saying to me, "I am right with you and I am staying with you in this hard time." Just as Noah was being born, Matt saw a huge rainbow in the sky. At the time I didn't really appreciate the information! But afterward, when Noah was really ill in intensive care, I read a verse from Genesis 9 that said God put a rainbow in the sky as a sign of his promise to Noah (see vv. 13-17). I felt God used this verse to reassure me that Noah was going to be okay.

Miraculously our little boy recovered, and we eventually moved into the house that had caused so much stress. I have consistently found in my life that when I turn to God and His Word, He gives me guidance, and even if it doesn't seem so at the time, He makes my paths straight (see Prov. 3:6).

THE TRUTH WILL SET YOU FREE

When I was offered the chance to write this book, I jumped at it, not only because I am passionate about encouraging young women in their faith, but also because I believe the Bible is true. I've experienced it to be true. I hope this book can somehow help to pass on the amazing goodness of God and the wonderful comfort and truth that the Bible brings. For the Bible is not just a textbook, a history book or some sort of Christian self-help manual. It is a powerful weapon in our hands—a sword for truth, freedom, light and life—and it was written for you (see Heb. 4:12)! So take it off the shelf, blow away the dust and put it to the test.

Read on and rise up as a girl of truth!

CHAPTER 1

THE TRUTH ABOUT IDENTITY

"I like me! I like me! I like me!" said Maisey as she marched around the kitchen with the sort of confidence only a two-year-old possesses. We laughed as we watched her dancing around singing such a happy song. "Mommy, I like me," she said once more before skipping off into the next room. I don't know where this statement came from, but it was sweet to hear what a great self-image our little girl had.

But how long would it last? In the summer, our little Maisey wanders round the garden splashing in the paddling pool and playing with her dolls. Her little bottom wobbles as she contentedly skips around without a care in the world. But what if one day she looks down and suddenly doesn't like what she sees? What if she stops "liking me" and wants to start "changing me"?

WHERE DOES YOUR WORTH COME FROM?

Recently we went to a friend's baby dedication. Levi Jesse Johnson was only 10 days old. He lay in his stroller blissfully unaware of all the attention he was getting. I looked across at him and smiled. He was a blank piece of paper, a clean slate. Although his character, gifts and abilities had already been formed in the womb, his experiences from that day on would determine who he was and how he felt about himself.

I was pretty sure his life experiences were going to be good. Levi is blessed to have two amazing parents who love God and are kind, generous and fair. He also has two sisters and a brother who I know will love and protect him. His extended family is vast and overflowing with decent, godly people. I think he will turn out just fine.

Yet not everyone is as blessed as Levi. We don't choose the families we are born into. Even if our moms and dads are nice people, successful in life, or church leaders, that does not guarantee they will make good parents. Whether or not you realize it, the experiences you've had at home and with your parents will determine how you feel about yourself today. Someone who has received affirmation and encouragement from his or her family will be sure to have a healthy self-image and a strong sense of security, confidence and emotional stability. Mary Pytches says in her book *Who Am I?*:

> No family is perfect but a properly functional family is characterised by parental availability, good communication and uninterrupted loving. The results for the child of such a stable and safe childhood will be a healthy perception of the world and, most importantly, a healthy self-image. It is impossible to overstress the value of two parents who stay together, who commit to one another, who love their children, talk to them, have fun with them, discipline them and are there for them day and night. These experiences are more precious in a child's life than a nice car, expensive holidays and having the best toys.[1]

That is the ideal. But what if that upbringing has not been your experience? You may have parents who were constantly arguing and fighting. Your mom may have criticized you and put you down in front of others. Your dad may have been absent. Some parents create such high standards for their children that many will have a huge fear of failure and live with a sense of not being good enough. Good grades equal pleasure and praise. Failure equals anger and rejection. Competition and comparisons may exist among siblings, and in such an environment, feelings of worthlessness may arise.

These are just a few of the harsh atmospheres that girls are growing up in today. Unfortunately, this is just the tip of the iceberg. Many more suffer from the bitter effects of divorce, bereavement, alcoholism, abuse and violence. Growing up in a home where you felt unsafe, unloved or unwanted will have a strong negative effect on how you relate to others.

Personally, my upbringing was a violent and rocky one. I have experienced difficulties and pain with each member of my family, which made me think that if my own family couldn't love me, why would anyone else? If even they rejected me, then I must be awful. This belief affected so many areas of my life, including my ability to make friends and feel secure in relationships. I thought that if my parents were to divorce, it would be a dream come true rather than a nightmare. However, when it actually happened, feelings of grief and the pain of having to choose between them caused me deep agony. My home was where I was hurt, but that's not how God intended it to be. Home should be where we receive lots of love and encouragement. If, like me, this was not your experience, you may have a negative picture of yourself. Without God's affirmation you will continue to feel unsure about who you are and what you can achieve. Unless you are helped to receive healing and hear God's truth, a low self-esteem can result, which can lead to all sorts of problems, including attention seeking, insecurity, clinginess, lying, eating disorders, depression, self-harm, addiction and a loveless void that leads many young girls to use their sexuality as a way to gain love and attention.

> ### Big Sister: *Mary Pytches*
> Five words changed my life forever!
>
> As long as I can remember, I had a private identity tag, which had put limitations on me. I was one of those happy "mistakes" born after my mother had finished—so she thought—having babies. Although I was loved by my family, I had always felt like an inconvenience, until I read these five words: "Therefore, as God's chosen people" (Col. 3:12). Suddenly it dawned on me—I may have been a mistake as far as my parents were concerned, but not to God. He had planned and purposed for me to be born.

EXAMINE YOUR SELF-WORTH UNDER THE MICROSCOPE

Take a look at the following questions:

1. Do you find it hard to receive a compliment?
2. Do you regularly compare yourself to others?
3. Do you become easily jealous of others?
4. Is there more than one thing you wish you could change about your body?
5. Are you continually putting yourself down?

If you answered yes to more than one of these questions, it is likely that you have a negative picture of yourself and are suffering from low self-esteem. How can you feel good about yourself again? Where should your sense of worth come from? I can still choose to live out of the old identity if I like, but from the day I was given an alternative, I began to choose it.

THE WORLD ASKS IF YOU MAKE THE GRADE

The lines grow long for the latest reality TV show. Girls practice for ages and shop for hours to achieve the perfect look. They give it all they've got and proudly show off what they believe is their God-given talent. But the judges aren't impressed. "Sorry, you're too fat," they say. "Who told you that you could sing? If I were you, I'd have stayed in bed, love."

Nice! Scrutinized, ripped to shreds, put down and rejected. Your five minutes of fame are over. Programs like these have us glued to our seats. Three executives sit in judgment. The rest of us sit back and relax. We have become obsessed with finding the winners and losing the wannabes.

Fame is seductive, and we can't deny that we've all wanted it at some point. From the age of three, I was singing into my hairbrush and performing in front of my mirror. I was in bands and singing regularly from the age of 14; then at 18 I had my first showcase. A producer from a small record company came to hear us play. At the end of our set, he sat down with the manager and went through why we wouldn't make it. To start with, he said I needed to lose weight and that I wasn't pretty enough. The others got a similar critique, and we went home via the kebab shop—pretty depressed! To be told my dream was over because I basically was too fat and not pretty was horrible. The worst thing was that I had always thought those things about myself, but hearing a complete stranger say it was like a punch in the stomach.

If the requirement for fame is being superskinny, sexy and drop-dead gorgeous, then I don't think many of us will make it on our own. Beauty in the eyes of the world is so narrow that it comes as no surprise that the door to eating disorders and low self-esteem is wide open. As we flip through our magazines, the images we see are not teaching us anything good about ourselves. The girls look stunning and slim; they are great clotheshorses. But the more we look at them the more we feel unsatisfied with ourselves. Someone somewhere is projecting to us that this is what we should look like. What depressing pressure.

WE GET OUR VALUE FROM SOMETHING WE ALREADY HAVE— A HEAVENLY FATHER WHO LOVES US— NOT FROM SOMETHING WE'LL NEVER HAVE, LIKE A PERT BUM AND GREAT BOOBS!

GOD SAYS THAT YOU ARE GOOD ENOUGH

As Christians we have a refreshing alternative. When we follow God, we have the option to be content with who we are. When we look at Him and fix our eyes on Him, we start to think about "good" rather than "food." We get our value from something we already have—a heavenly Father who loves us—not from something we'll never have, like a pert bum and great boobs!

The Bible tells us we will not be scrutinized or rejected on the basis of our outward appearance:

The LORD does not look at the things man looks at. Man looks at the outward appearance, but the LORD looks at the heart (1 Sam. 16:7).

YOU HAVE A NEW
IDENTITY IN CHRIST

Again and again our identity will be shaken unless we know, and can depend on, the indestructible, unchangeable truth of who we really are in the eyes of almighty God. As we seek to build up our identity on the truths of Scripture, we need the Holy Spirit to reveal the truth to our hearts. Have you ever heard someone say that your identity is in Christ but not known what it meant? This is a fundamental truth in our Christian lives—without grabbing hold of it and fully understanding it, we are not complete. In the following verses, God reveals our unique inner beauty:

> God spoke: "Let us make human beings in our image, make them reflecting our nature." God looked over everything he had made; it was so good, so very good! (Gen. 1:26,31, *THE MESSAGE*).

> You formed me in my mother's womb.... Body and soul, I am marvelously made! (Ps. 139:13-14, *THE MESSAGE*).

> God's Spirit touches our spirits and confirms who we really are (Rom. 8:15, *THE MESSAGE*).

Your mom may say you were an accident and you may feel you wish you hadn't been born. Or it is easy to feel trapped in a sister's or friend's shadow. You may sometimes feel ugly and inadequate, asking, "What are my giftings? Am I actually good at anything?" God can answer these questions and resolve our feelings of inadequacy. We belong to Him and He loves us. We don't need to get on a downward spiral of despair. As girls of God, we have Jesus to intervene personally and rebuild us by speaking the truth to us.

If you still find this hard to believe, there are practical ways to remind yourself to receive His truth. When I am ill, the doctor prescribes the right medicine to get rid of my pain. I pop my pills as prescribed until my symptoms go away and I feel better. Similarly, if we are feeling low and insecure, we need to read the Bible till we feel better.

A while ago someone said something really awful and untrue about me. I was totally crushed, but I had to make a choice. I could have dwelled on what the person said and believed it, but instead I simply took a verse from the Bible that was relevant to my situation and spoke it over and over again throughout the day until the cloud lifted. It lifted because I believed and received God's truth. If you struggle with your self-image, try putting one or two verses above your mirror so that every time you are tempted to look and feel worthless, you instead will be reminded of what God says about you.

The Bible talks about being transformed by the renewing of your mind (see Rom. 12:2). If we let Him, God will mold us into His image, renew our minds and restore our self-image:

You will know the truth, and the truth will set you free (John 8:32).

I want to finish this chapter with another extract from Mary Pytches's excellent book *Who Am I?*:

Nothing can change who we are in Christ, nothing can change our position in Christ, nothing can change the way our Heavenly Father sees us, or the affection He has for us. At the same time our distinctiveness is guaranteed. God knows us. Our names are written on the palms of His hands. Our tears counted. Every hair of our head is numbered. He calls us to Himself one by one and He gifts us individually. As if this was not enough we can rest in the knowledge that we are of utmost value to Almighty God. Not because of our performance or other people's opinion of us, but because we have been made in the image of God. Feeble, frail, ordinary human beings bear the imprint of the everlasting, All-powerful, One and Only God. The closer we walk with Him the more like Him we become. At the same time God has sealed our value by sending His beloved Son to die in our place. How much more can a Father do to prove we are of utmost worth to Him? All this will add up to an identity which is beyond comparison and will outweigh and outshine any ordinary human construction.[2]

Who am I then? I am a daughter, a sister, a student and a friend. I also am a precious, chosen, predestined, unique, loved and adored daughter of God.

CHAPTER 2

THE TRUTH ABOUT GIRLS AND GIRLS (FRIENDSHIP)

Research shows that loneliness is one of the biggest causes of depression in the U.K. All you want on a summer's day is to throw down a towel and compare tans with your friends. Who doesn't want a friend they can squeeze into the changing room with and ask, "Does my bum look big in this?" It's horrible to walk past the cinema and know that unless you go solo you're not going to see that chick flick you so desperately want to see. Who wants to live life like that? Being on your own is boring and makes life bland.

Girls need friends. We want to love and be loved, to laugh till we cry and to share our deepest hurts without the fears of back-stabbing and name-calling. Why is it that friendship can some-times be like holding sand in our hands? Before long it slips between our fingers and is lost forever. What is the secret ingre-dient to making and maintaining friends?

The ingredient is God. The reason our relationships fail and slip between our fingers is because we leave Him out of the equation. Without God our friendships can end up all catfights and catastrophes, but with Him we can go deeper and build a friendship that becomes a blessing. Believe it or not, the Bible can actually show us how to become better friends just by looking at the life of Jesus.

THE FACTS

Jesus is qualified to teach us how to live and cope with the joys and trials of relationships. He lived on Earth for 33 years. During that time, He traveled hundreds of miles and met thousands of people. In John 15:15, Jesus tells the disciples, "I have called you friends." In order to become the disciples' friend, Jesus first had to make Himself vulnerable, which made Him able to experience the joy of friendship.

But it wasn't all good. During His life He faced both extremes of human relationships. He knew what it was like to be seen as the leader of the in crowd, but He also knew how it felt to be mocked. Essentially, He went from being everyone's best friend to being the victim of a hate campaign. In both of these situations, Jesus was full of love and kindness. He pressed on to become the only perfect example we have of a true and faithful friend.

Like Jesus, we will experience the highs and lows of friendships. There will be times when the phone is ringing off the hook and our social calendar is looking more impressive than that of the most popular girl we know. There also may be times when we're pushed out of our friendship group and lied about by the people we trust. To learn to live in both situations, we must look more closely at the two extremes of popularity and unpopularity through the life of Jesus. How did He cope with being friendless and famous?

FRIENDLESS

Jesus ran into quarrels and fights because He stuck close to His values and stood up for what He believed. That meant He easily made enemies, because He would not be swayed or seduced into changing. Whether it was making friends with the out crowd or standing up for the outcast, Jesus was just not up for being in!

What made Him unpopular?

1. His Friends Were Unpopular

In Luke 19:1-10, we find Jesus passing through Jericho. Neighborhood chatter meant that soon a crowd would gather to meet Him. A little man with a big name and a bad reputation climbed a tree to get a better view of Jesus. That little man was Zacchaeus. He was a chief tax collector, and he was well known for giving people fines when they didn't deserve them. Just as we tut and mumble under our breath when we see a stingy police officer putting a ticket on our windshield, people muttered and whispered when they saw Zacchaeus out and about with his money bag. He was extremely unpopular, yet Jesus called him down from the tree and invited Himself to Zacchaeus's house for dinner. The crowd muttered in disgust, "He has gone to be the guest of a 'sinner'" (Luke 19:7). His choice did not please His fan club. However, Jesus was not out to impress; instead, He saw that Zacchaeus was a man who needed God. He reached out and showed kindness and friendship. Zacchaeus converted and actually promised to give back four times the amount he stole.

It would be easy to understand why we should stay clear of the troublemakers and the mean-minded. However, if we are to follow Jesus' example, then hanging out with them might not pollute us but in fact might affect them and change their ways forever!

2. He Was Different

If you don't want to stand out, then put on your baseball cap and keep your head down. If you want to avoid a fight, you'd better stay quiet. However, if you want to be true to who you are and what you believe, sometimes you have to lift up your head and speak out. Jesus wasn't afraid to do this—even when it made Him unpopular. He refused to be a crowd-pulling people pleaser. Instead, He chose to stick to the message of truth and hope, and the people flocked to Him. He wasn't afraid to risk losing friends because of who He really was.

In the campaign before an election, presidential candidates trek around the country like wannabes. Kissing babies, hugging grannies and patting dogs, they say what everyone wants to hear, grinning for the press and hoping they've impressed. Jesus wasn't a smooth talker on a popularity quest. He kept it simple: Follow the hard truth or walk away. Love me or hate me, this is who I am. I am God.

Sometimes we feel pressure to fit in and say nothing, but if we really have committed our lives to God, surely He is worth speaking up for. Being different is not bad; it is bold!

3. He Stood Up for What He Believed

A woman was about to be stoned to death (see John 8:3-11). In those days it was not an uncommon punishment—adultery was a serious crime. Yet Jesus stepped in and stood up for her. The crowd that gathered could easily have turned on Him. He chose to risk His own life to protect her from their judgment and her death sentence. He used His life to speak the truth and stamp out injustice.

In my class at school there was a girl named Frances. She was slightly odd looking and she tended to make things up. She was an easy target for the bullies. They ridiculed her and excluded her. Even when I knew it was wrong, I didn't stand up for her. I worried that if I stepped in maybe they would hate me, too. She endured four years of torment and one day she had had enough. She forfeited her education and left school because she could not bear it anymore. I often think about her. It was easy to do nothing, but I will always regret it. Jesus challenges us to stick up for the bullied, broken girls we see every day at school—not to back off, but to stand alongside and be a friend. Don't ask what you can gain; ask what you can give.

FAMOUS

Jesus had a group of 12 friends who followed Him everywhere. He also drew crowds so large that He once was forced to get into a boat and row across the lake just to get some space.

There is nothing better than knowing you belong and are liked. Deep down we all want to be popular and be part of the in crowd. Funny, outgoing people tend to draw crowds and be popular. What did Jesus have that made Him such a crowd-puller? What made Him popular?

1. He Was a Servant

Even though Jesus was God's Son, He was a servant. Maybe that doesn't sound too ridiculous. But just imagine if Prince William were at a public engagement in your area, and as he was meeting the crowds, he spotted some dog poop. However, instead of ignoring it, he got a pooper scooper and got rid of it! That would be a disgusting and lowly thing for a future king to do—such an act would never be carried out by royalty.

As God's Son, Jesus should have received the red-carpet treatment and had servants on hand to meet His every need. Astonishingly, He "did not come to be served, but to serve" (Matt. 20:28). He washed the disciples' feet (see John 13:5)—as sandal wearers they would have been covered in dirt and camel poop. And after He rose from the dead, He cooked them break-fast. He put their needs ahead of His own. What can we learn from this?

I doubt your friends would appreciate your offering to wash their feet, but there are other ways of putting them first. For example, how many times have you found out that you and your friend fancy the same guy? That always seems to happen to good friends. Maybe it's because they both have good taste! Yet it can end up ruining friendships. If you find out he likes you, don't just think, *Stuff it, girlfriend*, and go for it. Think about how you would feel if that happened to you! Serve your friend by waiting until she is over him and then triple-checking that she is cool with your dating him. If she is over him and she's your friend, then she should be cool. He might even have a nice friend you can set her up with!

2. He Was an Encourager

Jesus built His friends up, and when they were worried, He spoke words of encouragement and comfort. When your friends are down or upset, instead of just saying, "There, there" or "Give me a hug," why not find a verse from the Bible to help them? Words are cool, but sometimes a bit of God's truth is just what we need to hear. Let's invest something of value into our friends.

3. He Accepted Others

Jesus' friends were not perfect. When you look at the 12 disci-ples, it is easy to feel sorry for Jesus—they certainly had their flaws. Peter disowned Him, Judas was a thief who eventually betrayed Him, and James and John's nickname was Sons of Thunder, because they had such bad tempers (see Matt. 26:14-16,33-35,47-49,69-75; Mark 3:17).

If our friends are anything like us, they will have their flaws, too! It's not nice to be let down, especially by someone you trust.

And a friend who persistently lets you down is hard to stick by. In the Bible it talks about "bearing with one another in love" (Eph. 4:2). If we are going to be good friends, it is important we remember this verse. Friendship requires patience.

To Argue or Not to Argue— That Is the Question!

When we encounter fallouts with friends, the Bible shows us exactly how to resolve things and make up, not break up.

1. Resolve Things as Quickly as Possible

"Do not let the sun go down while you are still angry" (Eph. 4:26). When someone has hurt us, the more time we have to think about it, the deeper the hurt goes. We replay it in our heads again and again. We read between the lines—all the things they didn't say and all the things we should have said. Our stomachs churn. It hurts and it won't go away. We want revenge! We lay in bed replaying it once more: *If only I could see her now, I'd get her back and tell her what I really think of her. And I'm not the only one—loads of people think this, too. I can't wait for tomorrow!*

IF YOU WANT TO SORT THINGS OUT IN A GODLY WAY, SORT THEM OUT QUICKLY.

The problem with stewing is that it produces more anger. "I just need some space from you!" we say. Yet when we get space, we tend to use the time to think about it more rather than get over it. The more we think, the angrier we become. Oh, dear, what a messy cycle!

God in His wisdom tells us that when we have been hurt, we are not to let an evening pass. Nighttime is dangerous. It is when the plotting is done. We are alone with our thoughts, and things get nasty!

If you want to sort things out in a godly way, sort them out quickly. A moody text message, an emotional appeal to an answering machine or a note passed via a friend is just not good enough. Go directly to your friend. Don't let it fester, and don't let their sin cause you to sin. Sort things out today!

2. Resolve Things as Quietly as Possible

If a fellow believer hurts you, go and tell him—work it out between the two of you. If he listens, you've made a friend. If he won't listen, take one or two others along so that the presence of witnesses will keep things honest, and try again. If he still won't listen, tell the church. If he won't listen to the church, you'll have to start over from scratch, confront him with the need for repentance, and offer again God's forgiving love (Matt. 18:15-17, *THE MESSAGE*).

Here we have it in black and white! When we are tempted to run off and gossip to the class about what a no-good our friend is, we are stopped in our tracks by the truth. "Work it out between the two of you," or as the *New International Version* of the Bible says, "[Keep it] just between the two of you" (Matt. 18:15).

Proverbs 16:28 says, "A gossip separates close friends." There is no need to involve anyone else. I know it is tempting and actually quite therapeutic to conduct a venting session, but there really is nothing worse than off-loading to your other friends without first making an effort to go to the person who has wronged you. How will she know if you don't say? A gentle confrontation also can simply highlight a misunderstanding on your part. So many times I have found that a tiny misunderstanding can spark off a huge feud.

Sometimes when we do say how we feel, our honesty can actually make the friendship stronger and help someone be a better friend.

3. Learn How to Do It

Proverbs 27:6 says, "Wounds from a friend can be trusted." As calmly as possible and without aggression, it is best to explain clearly what it is your friend has done to hurt you and how it has made you feel. Avoid making big, accusing statements like "You make me feel . . ."; "You always . . ."; "You never . . ."; "I'm not your friend anymore . . ."; or "Amy's a better friend than you'll ever be!" Believe me, they won't help!

On the other hand, please don't feel bad about your feelings. I know people who end up apologizing for the person rather than letting him or her own up to the responsibility. Try starting with this: "Abi, I want to chat with you because I'm feeling a bit hurt. Yesterday we arranged to walk home together but you didn't turn up. I waited for half an hour, and when I rang your mom on my cell, she said you'd walked back with Sarah and the others. I felt upset, Abi. I waited for you for so long because we made an arrangement. I kept that arrangement, and it feels like you have let me down because you had a better offer. Can you tell me what happened?"

Hopefully, if Abi is a good friend, she will be humble and say she's sorry, or at least explain if there was a misunderstanding. If she turns around and says, "Back off! I can walk home with whomever I want," or makes an obvious excuse like, "I phoned your cell a thousand times, but it just rang and rang," you then have every right to bring along one or two other friends to try again to sort it out.

Please bear in mind though that there is nothing worse than a group of girls ganging up on a solitary chick. If your gang is yelling at her and accusing her, it will make it even harder for her to apologize. Stay calm and maybe just bring one friend with you whom Abi trusts, and then gently explain again how she hurt you. No matter how right you think you are, gentleness is the best response. Don't forget, you are trying to offer God's forgiving love, not hate and condemnation. If all else fails and you think it is necessary, perhaps you could ask your youth leader or an older friend to try and help you sort it out.

It is worth working through pain and misunderstanding if it means you have a friend at the end. It is better to be a servant and have a few really close friends than to be at the center of the in crowd and yet not be able to be yourself. Loneliness is a killer. Friendship is a gift.

Let's give to others what we would hope to receive. As we lean on God and ask Him to help us, we will begin to supply a type of friendship that the world cannot give.

CHAPTER 3

THE TRUTH ABOUT GIRLS AND BOYS (RELATIONSHIPS)

The first time I saw him he was standing outside, talking in the rain. My heart jumped and I quickly but casually asked a friend who this guy was. She informed me his name was Matt Redman and he worked at the church we were visiting. Fortunately, it wasn't long before I got to know Matt through a mutual friend and we started singing together in the worship band. As I saw more and more of Matt, I realized he was not only incredibly nice to look at, but he was also an amazing, kindhearted man of God. My heart fluttered and I blushed at the thought of seeing him again, but I sadly faced up to the reality that this gorgeous specimen and I would never be an item! Not only did we live miles apart, but we also were both pretty settled and content, and I could tell that Matt was not really interested in relationships. I got on with life and had no choice but to leave it with God. After two years of friendship and not being able to eat in each other's presence, we confessed our feelings and started going out. Eighteen months later we got married at the church where we originally met!

It's a romantic and almost perfect story. I met and married someone who loved me and was totally committed to God, and whom I adored and respected. Our relationship was aboveboard and godly—just how I'd dreamed it would be. It was the first time I'd ever had a relationship like it. Before meeting Matt, when it came to the opposite sex, my life was full of big mistakes and horrible dramas. Like many young girls, I was a bit giddy when it came to guys! Instead of drawing diagrams in biology, I was sketching wedding dresses. I remember lying on my bed one night and putting together a very long prayer, or wish, list. The list contained the preferred height, appearance, humor, character, career and godliness of my future husband. I knew what I wanted, and my standards were high.

Many of you may dream about what it will be like to meet the right one. No doubt thoughts of romance, marriage and companionship flutter through your head on a fairly regular basis. The important thing to remember is that this isn't wrong. In her book *Wait for Me*, Rebecca St. James writes:

> I believe that God has placed "The Dream" inside each one of us, unless he has specifically called you to singleness. We have a desire for intimacy, for someone to know us fully and love us completely. We long to be able to share our hearts and still find acceptance. A guy longs to protect; a girl longs to be protected. And that's exactly the way God created us. When we follow his plan, there are great blessings in store.[1]

God says:

> "For I know the plans I have for you," declares the LORD, "plans to prosper you and not to harm you, plans to give you hope and a future. Then you will call upon me and

come and pray to me, and I will listen to you. You will seek me and find me when you seek me with all your heart" (Jer. 29:11-13).

THE FACTS ON SEX

Why is it that with every good intention to live the fairy tale and get it right, we so often get it wrong? To start, the pressure is huge. The average age that girls have their first sexual experience is getting lower and lower each year. Research shows this is caused by children constantly reading about sex in magazines and seeing sex implied or acted out in sitcoms, films and soap operas. Many advertisements and billboards contain strong sexual undertones. Recently I was watching TV and was surprised to see a commercial for a leading brand of disinfectant that used sex to sell its product. After thoroughly cleaning the floor, the nice couple looked suggestively at the bottle and then glanced at each other before rushing upstairs to the bedroom. Maybe there really are people out there with hygiene fetishes and I was just missing something! Nevertheless, it was shocking to see sex so nonchalantly used to sell a household cleaning product.

Another factor is that psychologists reckon girls mature much earlier than boys. Dr. Nick Barlow, a consultant pediatric psychologist at Leicester Royal Infirmary, said:

At eleven, girls are leaning more towards adulthood, while for boys puberty is still a couple of years away. At this age boys don't have the same level of adolescent bonding and understanding as girls. Research shows that eleven-year-old girls talk a lot about boys—whereas boys of a similar age won't discuss girls at all.[2]

As early as 11, girls are tackling romance, whereas boys are focusing on skateboards and practicing magic tricks. The inevitable outcome of girls' maturing more quickly than boys, and being exposed to sex early on, is that experiencing sex during adolescence feels normal; it's totally insane to want to wait till marriage.

Therefore, we can't afford to be wishy-washy or borderline. The Bible spells out the place for sex:

> There's more to sex than mere skin on skin. Sex is as much spiritual mystery as physical fact. As written in Scripture, "The two become one." Since we want to become spiritually one with the Master, we must not pursue the kind of sex that avoids commitment and intimacy, leaving us more lonely than ever—the kind of sex that can never "become one." There is a sense in which sexual sins are different from all others. In sexual sin we violate the sacredness of our own bodies, these bodies that were made for God-given and God-modeled love, for "becoming one" with another. Or didn't you realize that your body is a sacred place, the place of the Holy Spirit? (1 Cor. 6:16-19, *THE MESSAGE*).

> Among you there must not be even a hint of sexual immorality, or of any kind of impurity, or of greed, because these are improper for God's holy people (Eph. 5:3).

The Bible's guideline is to keep it pure in our relationships and ultimately to have no sex before marriage. In fact, even a hint is wrong. For Matt and I this guideline answered the question of what we could touch when we were going out. We felt that anything other than holding hands and kissing was more than "a hint." However, for some young girls, even kissing may be too much too soon. This topic is a good one to talk through with your youth leader or your parents. Some people think their relationship is the exception because they aren't having casual sex, but we must be humble and accept that God knows best and He designed sex for marriage. Anything outside of that is not God's will. Many of our friends and peers may have the attitude that experimenting with sex is healthy and normal, but that's not right for us as girls of God. In this enormous and hugely sensitive issue, God has something of great worth to say to us, a very different message of truth and grace. Here are some verses to point you in the right direction:

> Run from anything that stimulates youthful lust. Follow anything that makes you want to do right. Pursue faith and love and peace, and enjoy the companionship of those who call on the Lord with pure hearts (2 Tim. 2:22, NLT).

> Nothing in all creation can hide from him. Everything is naked and exposed before his eyes. This is the God to whom we must explain all that we have done (Heb. 4:13, NLT).

> But remember that the temptations that come into your life are no different from what others experience. And God is faithful. He will keep the temptation from becoming so strong that you can't stand up against it. When you are tempted, he will show you a way out so that you will not give in to it (1 Cor. 10:13, NLT).

> It is God's will that you should be sanctified: that you should avoid sexual immorality; that each of you should

learn to control his own body in a way that is holy and honorable, not in passionate lust like the heathen, who do not know God; and that in this matter no one should wrong his brother or take advantage of him. The Lord will punish men for all such sins, as we have already told you and warned you. For God did not call us to be impure, but to live a holy life (1 Thess. 4:3-7).

Honor marriage, and guard the sacredness of sexual intimacy between wife and husband. God draws a firm line against casual and illicit sex (Heb. 13:4, *THE MESSAGE*).

No matter how deep the stain of your sins . . . I can make you as clean as freshly fallen snow. Even if you are stained as red as crimson, I can make you as white as wool (Isa. 1:18, *NLT*).

Create in me a pure heart, O God, and renew a steadfast spirit within me (Ps. 51:10).

THE PATHWAY TO PURITY

I do not want this chapter to come across as a heavy Christian rule book full of "don't do this, don't touch there" quotes. In fact, I would much rather encourage girls to focus on Jesus and be committed to Him. First John 2:15 (*THE MESSAGE*) says: "Love of the world squeezes out love for the Father." The more we concentrate on God, the more, I am convinced, we will become less and less distracted and enticed by worldly things. In reality there is a real need for godly truth and wisdom.

The world shouts loud and clear that experimenting with lots of different partners is completely healthy, natural and normal. I want to tell you now that this is a total and absolute lie. In the Bible the devil is described as a liar. He comes to "steal and kill and destroy" (John 10:10) and turn something that God designed to be beautiful into something sinful and dirty. It is totally false to think we can do what we please and not be affected.

If I told my daughter that huge amounts of sugar were good for her and if others told her the same thing, she would believe it was true. She also would have no problem or a guilty conscience if she ate lots of it all the time. To begin with, she wouldn't know it was wrong, because my lie tasted so good. How could something that tastes so good be bad for us? Sooner or later, though, the effects would be numerous: rotten teeth, diabetes, high blood pressure, heart disease, obesity and so on.

Do you see what I'm saying? The more we look at the subject of sex and relationships, and examine what is supposedly harmless, the more we see that we are living out the repercussions of a total lie. The effects are painful and sometimes disastrous: shame, insecurity, heartache, rejection, disease, adultery, unwanted pregnancy, abortion and the list goes on and on.

> **GOD SAYS THE PLACE FOR SEX IS INSIDE CHRISTIAN MARRIAGE. THE FRUIT OF THIS WISDOM IS A LIFE OVERFLOWING WITH LOVE, TRUST, SECURITY, WHOLENESS, FREEDOM AND JOY.**

God says the place for sex is inside Christian marriage—one man and one woman for life in a loving and committed relationship to each other and to the Lord (see Heb. 13:4). Of course, to some this seems pathetic, laughable and very old-fashioned; but the fruit of this wisdom is a life overflowing with love, trust, security, wholeness, freedom and joy.

DEAR BIG SISTER

For the remainder of this chapter, I thought I'd call on the help of the girls on the Soul Sister board. Based at Soul Survivor Watford, Rachel, Andreana, Vicky, Ali, Bee and I meet regularly to pray and seek God for the conferences, day events and resources that Soul Sister sets up and puts on. All of the members are in their 20s, and when it comes to boys, they all are in different situations—single, dating and one almost married. I have watched them and known them; I believe they will answer the questions with integrity, not only because they have a heart to encourage and to speak truth, but also because they live it out. I hope you are refreshed by what these girls have to say.

Is it okay to have a boyfriend?
Rachel: Yes, of course.

Ali: Yes. If one day you want a husband, you first need to have a boyfriend. Dating is part of life and as long as we handle it well—honestly before God and being accountable to our friends—it can be really good for us. Also, having *a* boyfriend is different from having *one* boyfriend *after another*. If you find you can't be without one, it's time to start asking yourself some tough questions about your security and self-worth.

Is it okay to have a boyfriend who isn't a Christian?
Rachel: Can I dare to rephrase the question? I would want to ask not "Is it okay?" but "Is it best?" God wants the best for our lives. Going out with a non-Christian is not just an issue of values and sex before marriage but, more important, an ability to share life together. If you love worship, wouldn't it be best to worship with him? If God were speaking to you, wouldn't it be best if you could chat with him about it? How can someone who will take

such an important role in your life not understand or share with you your first love and priority—Jesus?

Andreana: What is okay and what is beneficial are two completely different things. It's okay to touch the oven when it's hot, but you can avoid the pain and consequences by choosing to walk away. I wouldn't advise it.

How far should you go? Why?
Ali: Do you want to see how far you can push it or how much you can get away with? Or are you truly wanting to honor God, your boyfriend and yourself in every aspect of your relationship? The less you do together physically, the more chance you have of not stepping over the boundaries and ending up in difficult situations. Additionally, it is more likely that you will respect each other and be able to be totally open with God about your relationship as a whole. A good relationship doesn't necessarily need to become a physical relationship.

Rachel: I would say kissing. I know it sounds boring, but sex (so people tell me) is an incredible thing and it should be treasured and not treated lightly. When boundaries are broken, it is far harder to keep them again. The further you go, the harder it is to stop. Keep yourself as pure as you can.

I am a Christian and I don't see why it is wrong for me to sleep with my boyfriend. We are going to get married, so what is the big deal?
Beth: A stumbling block for many Christians can be when two people who are in a loving and committed relationship have sex outside of marriage. To them nothing immoral or sinful is going on and it can be very offensive to suggest otherwise. The truth is that the Bible tells us it is wrong. It is important to submit all

areas of our life to God, not just the bits that are easy. Sleeping together may feel okay, but we must learn that obedience and submission are all part of what it takes to be a Christian. Jesus said we are to take up our cross and follow Him (see Matt. 16:24; Mark 8:34; Luke 9:23). That means that when we choose to follow Christ, we choose to die to what we want and think is best, and we begin to count the cost. Once we stop wrestling and surrender our will to Him, the rewards are sweet.

My friend and I both like the same guy, but I've just found out that he likes me. What should I do?

Vicky: Honesty is a really important part of friendship. Proverbs 24:26 says that giving an honest answer is a sign of true friendship. If you were to start going out with the guy and not tell your friend, that would not be an honest or caring way to treat her. Jesus says we should live fully in the light—nothing hidden. Therefore, I would recommend talking it over with her first and maybe praying about it together, too. Then if you did start going out with the guy, your friend wouldn't hear about it second-hand. I'd also recommend that you be fairly sure that you and this guy have a long-term future together; otherwise, it wouldn't be worth the risk of hurting your friend in the process. Maybe it's better to just enjoy your friendship instead.

Rachel: It depends how strong your feelings are. Do not risk a friendship for something shallow. However, I don't think that should rule out the possibility of a relationship. "Be devoted to one another in brotherly [sisterly] love. Honor one another above yourselves" (Rom. 12:10). Try to honor your friend no matter what happens. Be honest with her. Ensure that you talk to her first and don't let her find out what could be devastating news from someone else. And if you do end up going out, don't flaunt it in front of her—be sensitive, be sisterly!

**My best friend has started seeing a guy and has
totally dropped me. I am really hurt. She also has
started to change and not come to church as much.
Should I say something or just move on?**
Beth: Since you are best friends, hopefully you will want to see
your friend happy and in God's will. Sometimes being in God's
will means things change. No one likes change; we can experience feelings of overwhelming insecurity and jealousy when situations like these arise. Ask God to give you a peace about it and
see what happens. I wouldn't advise dropping her—that means
you both will lose out on something precious. You may need to
just accept her relationship and try to get to know her boyfriend
without feeling threatened. However, if you genuinely feel that
you are being treated unfairly, why not gently chat with your
friend? If she is unresponsive, keep praying and maybe ask your
youth leader for advice. In reality, this guy may not be bringing
out the best in her, and as her friend you need wisdom to know
when to say something and when to just pray. In either of these
situations, I think that if you sincerely want the best for your
friend, you will do the right thing.

Is it wrong that all my best friends are boys?
Vicky: When I was growing up, most of my friends were boys.
I found it okay, although when we got close, there often were
complications over whether one of us wanted to be more than
friends. Having some good girlfriends means you can have
close friendships without that complication! There also are
things it might not be appropriate to discuss with boys, so girls
could help you there. The Bible encourages us to "pursue righteousness, faith, love and peace, along with those who call on
the Lord out of a pure heart" (2 Tim. 2:22). Purity and a desire
to follow God are great qualities to look for in friends; thus,
their heart and attitude are more important than their gender.

But overall I would recommend a balance of male and female friends.

Ali: The question I would ask is, Why are all your best friends boys? Is it that you are the only girl in your youth group, or is it that you aren't comfortable around other girls? I think the ideal is to have a mix of male and female friends. They are good for us in different ways and one without the other means we miss out.

Andreana: I have many great guy friends, but it is only girls that can truly relate to the struggles and experiences I have as a girl. I think that so long as there is a healthy balance in your relationships, it is fantastic to have both. I also might suggest finding older girls or women to be in your life. There really is something to be said for people who have already lived this period of life.

**All my friends have boyfriends and I don't.
Is it wrong to hate being single?**
Ali: Jesus came that we would have life and have it to the full (see John 10:10). He wants us to enjoy life. Sometimes this is easier said than done, and if you hate being single, it's no good pretending you don't. Let's be honest: As you get older, there are times when being single is hard. As someone who has been single for a long (and I mean *long*) time, I believe that God wants us not only to enjoy this stage of our lives for however long it lasts but also to come to a place of being able to say, just as Paul does in Philippians 4:11, "I have learned to be content whatever the circumstances." This isn't always easy, but here are my top tips:

1. Ask God to help you be content and enjoy being single. God says that if we ask, we will receive (see Matt. 7:7-8); and He is more than willing and able to help you.

2. Make a choice not to wallow in your misery or allow yourself to get pulled into a pity party with your friends. Pick one or two close friends with whom you can be honest and pray, but also give them permission to shut you up when you moan too much (and we all do that).

3. Choose instead to concentrate on all the freedom you have as a single person. The grass always seems greener on the other side. One day you won't be single, and you'll never get this time with your girlfriends back.

Rachel: Singleness is a natural stage in every life's journey and should be embraced as a gift from God. There is a freedom in singleness. "An unmarried woman . . . is concerned about the Lord's affairs: Her aim is to be devoted to the Lord in both body and spirit. But a married woman is concerned about the affairs of this world—how she can please her husband" (1 Cor. 7:34). Make it your aim to be a girl devoted to God in body and spirit. Grab hold of every day God gives you and live it wholeheartedly. Don't waste years waiting until you have a boyfriend for life to start. God has plans for you now.

A TIME FOR EVERYTHING

There is pressure everywhere. Fashions come and go. But when you flip through your glossy magazines, it seems the ultimate fashion accessory is a boyfriend. I want to encourage you that there really is no rush. Song of Songs 3:5 says, "Do not arouse or awaken love until it so desires." Boys are great friends and a good laugh, but we never seem to be allowed to simply enjoy their friendship without someone stirring or whispering and trying to force us together.

On the other hand, there are those who say, "Don't have boyfriends." In fact, this is a stance some Christians take. Again, my advice would be to talk through these issues with people such as your parents and youth leaders so that you can discern how God wants you to approach this whole area. I would say this though: Enjoy your youth and the freedom of being single. Enjoy just hanging out in groups and getting to know both boys and girls in an open and relaxed environment rather than in an exclusive and intense way. Ultimately, honor God and seek Him, and at the proper time you will enjoy this gift. There is a time for everything, and everything is beautiful in its time.

CHAPTER 4

THE TRUTH ABOUT SHINING (EVANGELISM)

As we learn more about our true identity in Christ, we grow in confidence and security. Yet this new identity is not simply a comfort blanket—a cozy truth we snuggle up to in order to feel comfortable and warm. Yes, of course our healing and wholeness is for us, but it is not exclusively for us! God has told us we're to be the light of the world (see Matt. 5:14). Jesus came and lived as a man on the earth for 33 years. He taught the saints and preached to the sinners. After His death and resurrection, Jesus gathered the 12 disciples and commissioned them by saying two significant things: "Go and make disciples of all nations" (Matt. 28:19) and "I am with you always, to the very end of the age" (Matt. 28:20). Like the eldest child joining the family business, we have become junior partners in the firm. Jesus says to us, "Go and do what I have been doing. That is your job description here on Earth." He also says, "I am with you always by my Holy Spirit and I live in you. Wherever you go I am there" (see Matt. 28:18-20).

Jesus will not be visiting your school—appearing in the flesh to perform miracles and stand up for the broken. Neither will He go on a rock-music tour of the country to tell people the good news about God or the reality of heaven and hell. Instead

He says, "You are the light of the world" (Matt. 5:14). The only way people will meet Jesus face-to-face and in the flesh is through you! He calls us to be His hands—reaching out to the lost; loving, comforting, giving and sharing; and holding out His forgiveness, compassion and grace. He calls us to be His feet—taking the good news to people who don't know Him. For some this will even involve traveling to new places and taking the message to the nations of the earth. Above all we are to have His heart, the sort of compassion that moves us to act—loving extravagantly and showing mercy—a forgiving love that covers over a multitude of sins.

WHAT'S YOUR FLAVOR?

Let me tell you why you are here. You're here to be salt-seasoning that brings out the God-flavors of this earth. If you lose your saltiness, how will people taste godliness? (Matt. 5:13, *THE MESSAGE*).

When you hang out with people, you catch their flavor. They leave behind a certain taste—sometimes a bitter or sour one. We are called to leave a God-flavor behind. The Bible describes this flavor as "saltiness." A meal without salt is bland and tasteless. A little seasoning brings out the rest of the flavors and makes a delicious meal. When people hang out with us, they should be able to taste what God is like. If we are half-hearted, weak and ashamed of our faith, how will people hear about Him? If we are screwed up, unkind or promiscuous, why will people want to meet our Savior? If we are just like everyone else, how will they taste the difference? Christianity will not seem attractive. It will be a total turnoff, and if you're not careful, before long you will lose your God-flavor. Swearing, smoking and messing around with sexual stuff are all ways of saying with your life, "I'm not with You, God. I'm with them." Salt needs to be salty, or what use is it?

> You are the light of the world. A city on a hill cannot be hidden. Neither do people light a lamp and put it under a bowl. Instead they put it on its stand, and it gives light to everyone in the house. In the same way, let your light shine before men, that they may see your good deeds and praise your Father in heaven (Matt. 5:14-16).

Our faith can easily become our little secret—something we keep to ourselves and only dabble in on the weekend. It is surprising to think that many girls' friends have no idea they go to church, let alone that they are Christians. This verse is saying that we should stand up and be proud: "Let your light shine before men." If there is darkness and you happen to have a light, you don't hide it; you share it! You don't tuck it away and try to keep it for yourself.

A friend of mine said her most embarrassing moment was when her mom came to her school to give out Bibles. The game was up; her cover had been blown. Her friends started asking if she was a Christian, too, like her mom. On the one hand she was happy to go to church, but she also wanted that part of her life to be very separate from the life she had at school with her friends. Her embarrassment drove her to get as far away from the truth as she could. She returned some years later, regretting the wasted years spent hiding her lamp under a bowl. To continue in the Christian faith we need to learn three things from Matthew 5:14-16:

1. **Be colorful.** Because God is in you, you should be vibrant and colorful, not dull and bland. Many people live with the idea that Christians are boring, dull, life-

less and sad. No way! Show them Christ in the flesh—
vibrant and full of life. You have His life in you.

2. **Be confident.** It's easy to feel ashamed and afraid.
Being different sometimes means you'll get attention,
but God also can give you boldness. God is on your
side—with you and for you. You have nothing to be
ashamed of and no reason to deny who you are and
what you believe.

3. **Be consistent.** Because of your faith, people will be
watching you. They will look at you to find out what
God is like. If your words are not backed up by your
actions, you will not only appear hypocritical, but
you'll also confuse people's view of God.

How do we do it and where should we start? Clambering up
on the nearest table and declaring, "Jesus is Lord," is not the best
evangelistic approach. Instead of shouting it out, why not first
live it out? It's not always what you say you believe but what you
do because you believe that makes the biggest impact. As others
look at your life and see a difference in you, they'll be sure to ask
questions and want answers. As one wise person has said,
"Preach the gospel at all times, and if necessary, use words."

IT'S QUESTION TIME

As a school outreach worker, I've been involved in many classroom debates. I have witnessed many aggressive questions and
equally aggressive answers. I think the best approach is a gentle
one. Although many times I've been attacked for my beliefs, it
doesn't help to be defensive. The "I'm right and you're wrong"
approach won't convert anyone. A verse from the Bible that's
always helped me is Proverbs 15:1: "A gentle answer turns away
wrath." If things start to get heated, it's best to stress that this is

what *you* believe and you are not forcing it on anyone else. Too often we appear arrogant, telling people they need Jesus before they have said they want Him.

However, once the questions start coming—if we're caught off guard—it can be quite overwhelming. It's easy to get tongue-tied and end up saying something too strong, or worse, inaccurate. When I first started doing outreach work at schools, I spoke to an assembly and started to answer a question about where Jesus would hang out if He were alive today. Without thinking through the answer, I blurted out, "Jesus would be with the prostitutes." The entire school hall—500 pupils and their teachers—erupted with laughter. What I had meant to say was that He'd be with the social outcasts and the needy, but what actually came out made Jesus sound like a dirty old man. I tried to explain what I meant, but no one heard me because they were laughing too hard. I don't think I did the Christian faith any favors that day!

In all, I worked for seven years as an evangelist in schools. During this time I traveled throughout the U.K. with four different Christian organizations and spoke to thousands of young people between 11 and 18 during classes and assemblies. Wherever I went young people seemed to ask the same questions. Just in case your friends are asking you the same things today, I have included a list featuring the most frequently asked questions and the answers we gave. The responses are only a rough guideline, but I hope they'll help should you ever find yourself on the spot and lost for words.

1. What is a Christian?

A Christian is someone who believes in God and in His Son, Jesus Christ. The earth didn't begin with a random big bang, nor did we evolve from monkeys. We believe that everything started with God. The story about this is in a book in the Bible called

Genesis. As Christians, we live our lives by what the Bible says. We find out from the Bible that God sent His Son, Jesus, to the earth. We do not need to argue His existence—historians have already proved it. In fact, there is more historical evidence to prove Jesus' existence than Julius Caesar's. Therefore, the argument is not *if* He existed but whether He was who He said He was. He claimed He was God's Son. As Christians, we have weighed up the evidence and put our beliefs and the Bible to the test, and found Him to be real.

2. Do you have to go to church?

If someone were a real fan of of the Los Angeles Lakers, he or she would make sure to attend all the games. The person wouldn't have to be dragged off to the Staples Center kicking and screaming. He or she would happily go along because of his or her love for the team. It is the same for us. Because we love Jesus and we want to know more about Him, we go along to church. We don't *have* to go; we *want* to be there.

3. What happens at church? Is it boring?

Normally there is some singing. We call that bit the worship. The type of music depends on what sort of church you go to. Some churches have DJs and dancers during the worship, while others use a more traditional style, like organ music and a choir. Where I go to church there is a really funky band with singers and modern music. We sing upbeat songs rather than hymns. There is a bit of praying and often someone will read a verse from the Bible. After the worship there is a talk about God. This part is helpful as it sometimes relates to stuff we go through at school, or it can teach us a bit more about Jesus and the Bible. When it's all over, we hang around for refreshments and a chat with our friends. Because I'm totally into God, I don't find it boring.

4. Why do you believe in God if you've never seen Him?

I've never seen the wind, but when trees blow and leaves fall, I know the wind exists because I've seen its effects. I haven't seen electricity either, but again I know it exists when I turn on the TV or the lights. I may not have actually seen God, but I've seen the effects He has on my life through prayer, the Bible and unexplainable things like healing (i.e., people getting better without doctors or medicine).

5. How do you know Christianity is true?

a. Simple trust. The most basic explanation is that I have put Christianity to the test and I have found it to be true. How will people who aren't Christians know if Christianity really works unless they put it to the test themselves? The Bible says bold things like, "Ask and it will be given to you" (Matt. 7:7). We can find out if statements like this are true by putting them to the test. For example, someone needs a job, so they read the verse and then pray, "God, please help me find a job near where I live. I trust You to do this because Your Word says, 'Ask and it will be given to you.'" Then what happens? They find a job within walking distance of their home. Of course, sometimes God answers our prayers in unexpected ways, because He knows better than we do what we *really* need.

> SOMETIMES GOD ANSWERS OUR PRAYERS IN UNEXPECTED WAYS, BECAUSE HE KNOWS BETTER THAN WE DO WHAT WE *REALLY* NEED.

Another example of seeing the Scriptures at work is evident when I'm feeling low and alone. Despondent, I pick up my Bible and my eyes fall on the words "The LORD is close to the broken-hearted" (Ps. 34:18). I pray, "Lord, thank You for telling me You are close to me; please help me to feel Your love, too." Suddenly, I am interrupted by a knock at the door. A good friend is passing by and feels she should tell me that God loves me. She comes in for a cup of tea. Not only do I feel totally encouraged, but I also am not lonely anymore!

God shows Himself to be real and true time and time again. Pass it off as coincidence if you like, but each of these examples is a real testimony to me that He is alive!

b. Deep faith. There are some things in my life that I don't understand. In each situation, I need to choose to have faith. Even if I still don't understand and the future looks bleak, I know God is in control and He will take care of me. Many times we see only half the picture. It is easy for panic and frustration to set in. Faith says, "I believe that God is for me and that He sees the whole picture." Therefore, faith enables us to wait patiently. As the Bible says, "My times are in your hands" (Ps. 31:15). We know God—our helper and defender—is looking after us. "My thoughts are not your thoughts . . . my ways [are] higher than your ways" (Isa. 55:8-9). In this verse from Isaiah, God is gently reminding us that we see things in part—from a small and limited perspective—but God sees the whole thing and is working in ways we don't see or understand.

6. If there is a God, why do bad things happen?

When God made us, He decided humans with free wills were much better than robots that did what they were told without a choice. There are two responses to free will. One is obedience; the other is rebellion. We can choose either to love God and follow Him or to turn away from Him and sin. He allows each of us this choice, and it gives some explanation as to why much of the world is in chaos. The whole of creation is on a course for destruction.

Society doesn't want anything to do with God until it all goes wrong. Then God gets blamed. Disasters, massacres, murders and wars are horrific acts of violence and rebellion. As Christians, we can pray against these things and ask God in His mercy to intervene.

7. Does God forgive murderers?

The Bible teaches us that "all have sinned and fall short of the glory of God" (Rom. 3:23). We all sin and deserve punishment. But through Jesus' death on the cross, we can experience the gift of forgiveness. If we truly repent (i.e., recognize our sin and say we're sorry), we can be forgiven. This goes for everyone—including murderers, bullies and thieves.

8. If I don't believe in God, does that mean I'm going to hell?

The Bible tells us that everyone will be judged. The Bible talks a lot about heaven and hell. As Christians, we believe that both of these places exist.

What is heaven? Heaven is eternity with God. God is good and heaven is all the amazing things about God under one roof—eternal peace and joy, and no more sadness or suffering. What is hell? Hell is eternity without God. Hell is everything God detests. It is filled with evil, greed, sickness, sorrow and suffering.

It isn't a case of goody-goodies go to heaven and murderers go to hell. Anyone who chooses to believe receives a place in heaven. For something so huge it seems so simple. By accepting Jesus, repenting and turning from our old lives to follow Him, we can go from hell to heaven. What an amazing destiny!

9. Does being a Christian mean that you can't drink or have sex?

Although drinking in moderation is acceptable for adults in some Christian circles, drinking in excess is clearly wrong. It leads to all sorts of things: loss of judgment, loss of inhibitions, loss of self-control and a lot of unwise, even dangerous, behavior. In extreme cases, an addiction is formed.

In all this we believe God knows what is best for us. If sex outside of marriage is good for us, why are the repercussions so bad? Hurt, rejection, sexual diseases, unwanted and teenage pregnancies and, worst of all, abortion, can all result from our carelessness. It's not just about the bad effects it has on us; it's about trying to be obedient to God. Because we have chosen to follow Him, we also choose to follow His ways. Even if it seems inconvenient or undesirable at times, that's part of a Christian's way of trying to honor God in his or her life.

10. Isn't Christianity just a load of rules and regulations?
We all need rules. Without rules we just would do what we wanted and end up suffering the consequences. God isn't bossy and boring; He is a wise and loving Father who knows what's best for us. When we see the guidelines God provides us in the Bible, we can be resentful and say, "Who are You to tell me what I can and can't do? I want to go out with that guy, sleep with him, drink and take drugs, and no one is going to stop me." Or our attitude can be one of love and obedience: "I accept that God's ways are better than my ways, and I choose to follow Him and not myself. I will not rebel or fight against my God. I love God, and because I also trust Him 100 percent, I know He has shown me the best way to live my life, and I am grateful."

LET THEM SAVOR YOUR GOD-FLAVOR

Yet being a Christian is not just about having the "right" answers. Your biggest challenge today is to live your life and not lose your saltiness. Christianity isn't about staying at home and trying to be "saintly." It is okay to go out with your friends, but make sure you take your God-flavor with you. Let them taste it by your consistently preaching the gospel with your life. When they see you making a difference, I guarantee they will ask questions. And when they do, be ready to answer honestly and boldly.

Remember God is with us on our journey. Sometimes God's power is most evident in our weakest and most vulnerable moments. Many times I have stood in front of a class of bored and annoyed-looking 15-year-olds and thought, *I just can't do this.* As I've stood up, my fear is apparent—red cheeks, sweaty palms and muddled words. There were some horrible moments: I was shouted at, laughed at and even spat on. But throughout all of the weakness and embarrassment, I experienced the overwhelming privilege of telling people about Jesus. I personally had the opportunity to hear their struggles and answer some of their questions. Most amazing of all, I witnessed hundreds make a first-time commitment to God. Lost and confused, hurting and alone, they found their Savior and went from hell to heaven. That is what our lives are all about!

We have the privilege of knowing Him. Someone somewhere showed us what He was like, and since then our life and our destiny have been changed forever. We have that same privilege to pass along: to show others what He is like and lead them to the Cross. It isn't a shameful duty; it is an inherited calling.

God is with us, helping us and changing us to be salty light bearers. I wouldn't want to be anything else!

CHAPTER 5

THE TRUTH ABOUT FORGIVENESS

(PART 1)

The amazing change that takes place when we become Christians starts right here with the subject of forgiveness. The truth is, we possess something we did not earn, could not buy and cannot even get our heads around.

In Luke 7:36-50, Jesus is invited to the home of a prestigious local leader, a Pharisee. During dinner the host plans to get time alone with Jesus, so he can figure out exactly what Jesus is up to. But right in the middle of the evening's proceedings, an uninvited woman bursts in. Sniveling and bawling, she falls at the feet of Jesus. Yes, it is every man's worst nightmare—a crying woman!

Her background is not an impressive one. We believe this woman is either a prostitute or someone who is known for some sort of sexual sin, possibly adultery. To everyone else at the dinner table, it is obvious who she is and what should be done with her. Eyebrows are raised as the supposed Godsend does nothing. The Pharisee turns down his nose and casts his judgment: Case closed—Jesus is a fraud. After all, if He is such a wise prophet, He would know what sort of woman sits at His feet. Any respectable leader would have her thrown out onto the street.

Of course, Jesus knows who this woman is, and so does she. She earns a reputation that she cannot shed. Disgraced and disliked, a hopeless case, she finds Jesus. His message of forgiveness and freedom overwhelms her and gives her hope. To be told she is clean is something she never thought would happen. To others, like the Pharisee, she will always be a dirty-rotten disgrace. Yet Jesus tells her, "Your sins are forgiven" (Luke 7:48), which provides her a new life to begin.

No doubt she weeps over the cruel judgments that her past earned her. But now in this Pharisee's front room, she finally tracks Jesus down and is overwhelmed with thanks. She brings an alabaster jar of perfume (rumored to be worth a year's wages) and pours it over His feet. And there she sits, without shame, weeping tears of relief, gratitude and awe. Who would know, apart from herself and Jesus, what actually is going on? To all around, it seems like an immoral display of lust and emotion. But this is her worship. She loves her Lord, and she comes to bow down and simply say "Thank You."

I relate to this woman's intense feelings of joy and gratitude for being forgiven and to her tendency to feel ashamed, especially when other people reminded her of her past. A few years ago, at a well-known Christian conference I attended with my husband, I bumped into a lady from my old church. I hadn't seen her for many years, and as I began to introduce Matt, she blurted out, "I bet Beth hasn't told you what she used to be like. I've got so many stories!" On and on she went telling story after story, laughing and thinking Matt must be enjoying these tales. I stood there biting my lip, trying not to cry. It hurt so much.

When I see people like this from my old school or youth-group days, I am tempted to hang my head in shame. The things I did as a teenager seem to have gained me a reputation that, even in my 20s, I cannot shed. Unfortunately, in their minds, I will always be that person, and the enemy would love to persuade me to live in that shame. Fortunately, I asked God for forgiveness and I have been forgiven and changed. I am no longer that person, so I don't have to live under that judgment or shame. The immature mistakes, the willful acts and the plain rebellion were all taken away from me when I became a Christian. I am free to be at peace with my past:

> If anyone is in Christ, he is a new creation; the old has gone, the new has come! (2 Cor. 5:17).

A NEW DAY

I was brought up to go to church and to believe in God. But even though I knew what I was taught was true—and I'd witnessed it to be real—I chose to do my own thing. I enjoyed taking part in church, singing and socializing, but my own life was far removed from what I'd heard preached at youth group and the words I happily sung along with at church. I was probably every youth leader's worst nightmare!

Some of the reasons for the way I lived outside of church were pain, insecurity, family problems and peer pressure. But at the end of the day, I'd never really given myself 100 percent to God. I hadn't experienced the amazing things that happen when you turn

> WHEN WE'RE HALFHEARTED ABOUT GOD, WE MISS OUT ON INCREDIBLE FREEDOM, FRIENDSHIP AND FORGIVENESS.

your back on the old life and you live for Him and He lives in you. I did not understand the power of prayer or the incredible way that the Bible brings light, truth and comfort to so many different situations. When I really turned around and stopped doing things I knew were wrong, I experienced the amazing sense of His forgiveness and a fresh start. This is when life for me truly began.

It says in John 10:10 that Jesus came that we may have life, and have it to the full. When we're halfhearted about Him—or, as Jesus put it, "lukewarm" (Rev. 3:16)—we stop ourselves from living in the fullness of God. We miss out on incredible freedom, friendship and forgiveness.

Things changed for me when I went to a Christian camp. No one there would have known my real state. At the start of the camp, even I would have considered myself a Christian. But the more time I spent with people who were truly on fire for God, the more I realized there was a massive difference between their Christianity and mine. Every evening someone would preach, and each time I felt more and more gripped by the truth, convicted that I'd never really chosen to follow God with a whole heart. I'd joined a fantastic social group based on something I truly believed in, but I chose to have the best (or rather worst) of both worlds by dabbling in both. I did what I pleased outside of church. I smoked and regularly got very drunk, and I also messed around with guys. As you can imagine, this gave me quite a reputation around the church and the classroom.

God in His grace has taken those things and wiped them out of my life. Like the moneylender (see Luke 7:41-43), He canceled my debts and wiped them out. Thus, at the age of 18, I had a fantastically clean slate—a brilliant plain page in front of me. All those labels—liar, tart, loser, hopeless case—were completely erased. Yet it does not mean those things never happened, nor does it mean that I haven't suffered consequences of my sin. I deeply regret the wasted years I spent drinking and throwing myself at boy after boy. I am gutted that when I was at school, I didn't stand up for God. But more than anything, I'm humbled that my God still received me. He gave His beloved Son, Jesus, who in dying on the cross took all my sins and buried them with Him. Then He rose again, and so did my new life in Him. Don't waste your youth on worthless sin—let God be glorified today!

REFRESHING TRUTH

As for you, you were dead in your transgressions and sins, in which you used to live when you followed the ways of this world and of the ruler of the kingdom of the air (Eph. 2:1-2).

But because of his great love for us, God, who is rich in mercy, made us alive with Christ even when we were dead in transgressions—it is by grace you have been saved (Eph. 2:4-5).

In him we have redemption through his blood, the forgiveness of sins, in accordance with the riches of God's grace that he lavished on us with all wisdom and understanding (Eph. 1:7-8).

As far as the east is from the west, so far has he removed our transgressions from us (Ps. 103:12).

What does this mean for you? It means that God does not want you to live your life beating yourself up, feeling ashamed and continually saying you're sorry for things He's already forgiven. The truth is that once you've said you're sorry and received His forgiveness, God says, "I remember your sins no more" (see Isa. 43:25).

Just as the east and the west will never meet, so your past sins will never be joined to you again. There is now a choice to make: Believe a lie and dwell on the past, or be like the woman in Luke 7 who received God's forgiveness and fell at Jesus' feet and worshiped. When the Bible says, "My grace is sufficient for you" (2 Cor. 12:9), it means God's forgiveness is enough for you and your life—whatever you've done. As a forgiven person, you are now free. Choose to receive this truth, and then enjoy living in the wonder of it.

CHAPTER 6

THE TRUTH ABOUT FORGIVENESS
(PART 2)

An envelope dropped on the mat. It was for me. I was only 18 and not used to receiving my own mail. I looked inside and could not believe it. "Mom! Guess what! I've won a competition!" In big bold letters it informed me that I was now £20,000 (around $33,000) richer! At this point excitement prevented me from realizing that somehow I'd won a competition I never actually entered. As naive as it must sound, I believed the letter, which stated I'd been "selected at random" and could now put my feet up and live off my undeserved earnings. Of course, I soon sobered up when I read the very, very small print. It stated that I would be required to send a small administration fee of £100 (around $166) to process my huge check. Apparently this was normal and should be done immediately or my winnings would be handed over to someone else. My common sense finally prevailed. I realized that the only prize I had won was "Bimbo of the Year." There was no £20,000 prize. Someone was just trying to make some fast cash, and I'd been taken for a ride!

You'd think I wouldn't be so stupid again, but only last year Matt and I received a mysterious letter. It was from a solicitor in Nigeria. Amazingly Matt was the sole beneficiary in the will of a minister who recently died. Apparently this man attended a meeting where Matt led some worship. Despite the fact he had his own family, he'd changed his will and decided Matt should have all his money. We were tracked down and informed of his sad and sudden death.

I'm sure you're thinking this was an obvious setup, but Matt and I were experiencing some money problems and I assured my husband this was our answered prayer. After much persuasion from me, Matt decided to e-mail the solicitor and find out a bit more about it. To our surprise, the reply stated that it was all legitimate and we were left nearly the equivalent of 1 million dollars. What a blessing!

Matt decided we should give it away or use it for the ministry. I decided we would have homes in London, Milan and Paris! Unfortunately, neither of these dreams came to pass. Soon after this we were in contact with Scotland Yard—discovering that we'd almost been taken on a huge fraudulent ride.

So Where's the Catch?

When we hear about God's grace, it is easy to think there must be a catch. After all, you don't get something for nothing in this world. You have to buy one to get one free, so it's not free after all, is it? But there really is no catch when it comes to grace. It's a free gift. Here's how one worship song describes it:

> The grace of God upon my life
> Is not dependent upon me,
> On what I have done
> Or deserved,

But a gift of mercy from God,
Which has been given unto me
Because of His love,
His love for me.

It is unending, unfailing,
Unlimited, unmerited,
The grace of God given unto me.[1]

Grace has fallen into your lap with your name on it, because that is how God decided it shall be. What you do with it is up to you.

Our Call to Duty

We can easily lead ourselves to believe that as Christians we *have* to be good and kind. We can feel it is our duty to be forgiving. The truth is that the Bible says we don't *have* to do anything:

If you are led by the Spirit, you are not under law (Gal. 5:18).

However, God does provide some guidelines: "Freely you have received, freely give" (Matt. 10:8). In the same way that we have freely and gladly received the gift of God's forgiveness, we are encouraged to freely give it away to others.

This is explained in greater detail in Matthew 18:21-35. Peter, one of the disciples, is fed up. He has been hurt by the same person yet again. He is coming to the end of his rope and starts to think that maybe the person doesn't deserve any more chances. Peter goes to Jesus and asks Him, "Lord, how often should I forgive someone who sins against me? Seven times?" "No!" Jesus replies, "seventy times seven!" (vv. 21-22, *NLT*).

Peter probably is thinking that to forgive someone seven times is quite gracious. Jesus responds by saying that 490 is a more acceptable number of times.

Obviously, this story is not about the times table. Jesus makes the point that we need to dispose of our tally-mark mentality and stop counting, and keep forgiving instead. Yet we stamp our feet and whine like a two-year-old, "Why should I?" Because that is how God has treats us.

> Therefore, the kingdom of heaven is like a king who wanted to settle accounts with his servants. As he began the settlement, a man who owed him ten thousand talents was brought to him. Since he was not able to pay, the master ordered that he and his wife and his children and all that he had be sold to repay the debt. The servant fell on his knees before him. "Be patient with me," he begged, "and I will pay back everything." The servant's master took pity on him, canceled the debt and let him go.
>
> But when that servant went out, he found one of his fellow servants who owed him a hundred denarii. He grabbed him and began to choke him. "Pay back what you owe me!" he demanded.
>
> His fellow servant fell to his knees and begged him, "Be patient with me, and I will pay you back."
>
> But he refused. Instead, he went off and had the man thrown into prison until he could pay the debt. When the other servants saw what had happened, they were greatly distressed and went and told their master everything that had happened.
>
> Then the master called the servant in. "You wicked servant," he said, "I canceled all that debt of yours because you begged me to. Shouldn't you have had

mercy on your fellow servant just as I had on you?" In anger his master turned him over to the jailers to be tortured, until he should pay back all he owed.

This is how my heavenly Father will treat each of you unless you forgive your brother from your heart (Matt. 18:23-30).

Our Need to Recognize Unforgiveness

Look again at the previous verses from Matthew 18 and notice just how forgiving the king was to his debtor. Reading it again makes me realize what a hypocrite I have been. Who am I to hold a small thing against my brother, sister or friend when God has forgiven me for so much big stuff? It's easy to allow little incidents of unforgiveness to finish off our friendships.

> WHO AM I TO HOLD A SMALL THING AGAINST MY BROTHER, SISTER OR FRIEND WHEN GOD HAS FORGIVEN ME FOR SO MUCH BIG STUFF?

One of my weaknesses is that I have a tendency to write people off. Because of my past, I sometimes overreact when people hurt me. My defense mechanism is to shut them out of my life. My heart says, *I let you in once and you hurt me, so I'm not going to let you do it to me again.* I close the door on that person with, *It was nice knowing you. See you later!*

Not only does this sort of reaction cause a nasty shadow to hang over me—because it constantly bugs me—but time and time again I have let my pride cause a small thing to ruin a great friendship.

Here are some ways to recognize the beginnings of unforgiveness:

1. **Lump in the throat.** Seeing this person or hearing about them unexpectedly can cause an immediate physical reaction. Something inside of us is saying, *I have a problem with this person.*

2. **Gossip.** If someone has hurt us, the quickest way to get it off our chest is to pass it on and gossip about that person. This can cause division in friendships and can be very harmful to both parties. If there is someone we are constantly wanting to run down (and it isn't necessarily just because of jealousy), we need to stop talking about that person. Instead, we need to go to the person honestly and gently. If that's not appropriate, we should take it straight to God. But as quickly as possible, we need to extend a little grace and forgiveness.

3. **Overreacting.** If we are easily upset and fly off the handle when a person's name is mentioned, our response shows that our feelings are having a hold over us and are causing us to be irrational.

4. **Grudges.** A few clumsy comments from a friend at school can easily build up and turn into a grudge. Eventually, each unforgiven slip will add up to one big grudge. Grudges destroy relationships because, as hard as we try to, we cannot enjoy a friendship when many hurt feelings run rampant under the surface. We can start by working out where the grudge actually started and pray it through from there.

5. **Bitterness.** Bitterness is scary because to have it we have allowed unforgiveness and grudges to exist for a while. The Bible talks about a "root of bitterness" that grows up and causes trouble (Heb. 12:15, *NKJV*). Like a small weed it spreads and gains control of a plant's solid and healthy foundations. Bitterness creeps in

and before long it has killed the whole plant. Bitter people are easy to spot. Warped and whiny, they view most things in a negative light and become touchy and insecure around cheerful and positive people.

Bitterness is an easy way for the enemy to ruin an otherwise healthy Christian. But just as a good gardener knows how to get rid of a lethal weed—no matter how much it has spread—God is able to free someone from the destruction bitterness brings. If we or someone we know is rooted down by bitterness, it is essential to get help soon.

6. **Revenge.** When we carry unforgiveness in our hearts, we want to see justice done; we want to see the person who has hurt us punished. Unforgiveness—and the anger it brings—gives us power over others. When we forgive, we lose that power. We give it to God and we are free. The hard part in all this is that while we have the choice not to sin, we don't always have the choice not to be sinned against. Very wrong things can happen to us. It is a reality that many young girls are abused, assaulted and mistreated by others—often by a family member. They find themselves having to deal with the consequences of someone else's evil, which unfairly has the potential to ruin or spoil their lives.

If this does occur, how do we get over it? We may wrestle with releasing forgiveness. After all, we did not ask for this to happen, and we certainly did not deserve it. Why should we have to forgive? *Surely forgiveness is letting them get away with it,* we may think.

"'It is mine to avenge; I will repay,' says the Lord" (Rom. 12:19). "For we must all appear before the judgment seat of Christ" (2 Cor. 5:10). These verses reveal that even if our hurts aren't resolved on this earth, they will be one day. Ultimately, God will judge and punish wrongdoers. Believing this and applying it to our situations brings peace and relief. God will win the battles for us.

HIS FORGIVENESS IS OUR RESOURCE

As you pray, know that the act of forgiveness does not condone what's been done to you. Instead, you are actually choosing to put it behind you. Forgiveness says, "I will not let this person, or their sin, dominate, control or rule me." You are choosing to give it to Christ.

We won't always feel we have the strength or ability to forgive. If you're finding it hard to forgive someone, why not start at the Cross? Examine all that Jesus has done for you, all that He has saved you from and how forgiven you are now. Then look again at your issue of unforgiveness. It's easier to forgive when you truly grab hold of how much you have been forgiven. Many times when I really have been sinned against, I have had to ask God to help me forgive. I simply cannot do it on my own. In our weakness, God will help us to be merciful and enable us to release forgiveness.

If the issue of unforgiveness is very difficult, approach a trusted friend or leader and ask them to pray about it with you. The main thing is not to let unforgiveness get hold of you. In the case of abuse (or other illegal acts), it is essential to find a Christian counselor who can help you to talk and pray it through. You cannot live with it alone.

Jesus was human. He showed us that He felt things as strongly as we do. Yet so often we can think of Him as a non-feeling God. When bad things happen to us, it's okay to feel angry. He felt angry. He also taught us how we should respond to anger. Paul said, "In your anger do not sin" (Eph. 4:26). Do not let what someone else has done to you cause you to sin against someone else and God.

God wants us to be free from the burden that unforgiveness brings—not to be bitter and angry forever. He wants us to bring our hurts to Him so that He can take them. The truth is that when we forgive, whatever has been said or done to us will no longer have the same hold on us. Jesus' truth speaks into our situation: "It is finished. Now go in peace. You are free!"

CHAPTER 7

THE TRUTH ABOUT DESTINY

If I were to ask you what your dreams are, I wonder what you would say? Maybe you sing, dance or act, and you long to use your gifts to tell people about Jesus. Perhaps you feel a calling to teach, train and disciple, or be a missionary and study and teach overseas. Maybe you simply long to be a wife and a mother one day. Whatever the difference in detail, the desire is the same: You have a deep longing and a far-off dream that bubbles inside and won't go away.

When I was a teenager, I absolutely loved singing. In tenth grade, everyone had an interview with a lady from the careers department. She rolled her eyes when I told her I wanted to be a singer. It didn't put me off, though. I was determined, and it was all I could think about. When I committed my life to God, my passion for singing remained, but my dream had a new focus. I wanted to use my singing to tell people about Jesus.

However, while I was confident with friends, I could not speak or sing in public without going red and having panic attacks! Every day when the teacher took roll, I dreaded having to call out, "Here, Sir." If I was picked to answer a question in class, I would look down and get a rash on my neck, which my friends fondly referred to as my "alien neck." Not only was I lacking in confidence, but I also knew that realistically there were many other singers who were heaps better than me. No way would I get picked over them. However, my desire did not go away, and I decided to keep on praying. If it was God's will, then He could make it happen and give me confidence.

After I properly committed my life to God, I lay on my bedroom floor trying to write a song. Yet all I could think about was the fact that I wanted to tell young people about Jesus. I prayed that God would enable me to do this and that He would open the doors, because I didn't know any way that this could happen. Two huge answered prayers later—in a matter of only two months—I was standing in front of hundreds of kids, talking and singing about God as an evangelist in schools. A friend of a friend was looking for a singer to join his band. The band did lots of gigs and schoolwork, and they asked my friend if they knew anyone who would fit the bill. I was astounded. I never thought God would use me. I hadn't been able to even answer my name in class, so how would I speak to a roomful of school kids?

YOU CAN DREAM WITH GOD

I learned a valuable lesson about God through this experience that I want to pass on to you. God wants you to dream big dreams with Him. He also wants to give you the opportunity to fulfill those dreams. The Bible clearly says that He will give you the desires of your heart (see Ps. 37:4). We follow a God who gives us gifts and abilities, so naturally we have a longing to use and develop those things. If you are blessed with the ability to sing, dance, act, lead worship, teach, nurture or care for others, that blessing has come from Him. We don't have to learn to live in frustration and put the things that we love on the back burner. We simply need to submit those things to Him.

In other words, my gifting is an entrustment—a gift God has given me to glorify Him. Of course, it's okay to enjoy doing the things we're called to, but the gift is never more important than the Giver of the gift. We need to keep checking that we're pursuing God ahead of our dreams.

Another lesson we can learn from the Bible is that we don't have to carry the burden of trying to make our dreams happen ourselves:

> What he opens no one can shut, and what he shuts no one can open (Rev. 3:7).

This verse gives me great confidence and has proved true in many lives. Even though we may have many practical or physical odds against us, God is able to open up opportunities and use us beyond our wildest dreams.

Of course, human nature says it will never happen—how on earth could it? All around you there are more popular and more talented people whose futures look much brighter than yours. If your classmates gave the title "most likely to succeed" to one of the students, would you be chosen? The chances are you would not. Worldly success is based on shallow things such as looks, wealth, popularity, status and charm, but the Bible says that a future with God is based on much deeper things:

> Brothers, think of what you were when you were called. Not many of you were wise by human standards; not many were influential; not many were of noble birth. But God chose the foolish things of the world to shame the wise; God chose the weak things of the world to shame the strong. He chose the lowly things of this world and the despised things—and the things that are not—to nullify the things that are, so that no one may boast before him (1 Cor. 1:26-29).

When God chooses His workers, the one thing that matters on their résumé is the state of their heart. Should we settle on the assumption that we'll be overlooked and our dreams will have to die? No way! Go to the Bible, which clearly says that God is the door opener (see Rev. 3:7). God has a plan for us (see Jer. 29:11). If His will is for us to do something and we are faithful, be assured that He will cause it to happen.

> **WHEN GOD CHOOSES HIS WORKERS, THE ONE THING THAT MATTERS ON THEIR RÉSUMÉ IS THE STATE OF THEIR HEART.**

Often disappointment and confusion come when we feel nothing is happening and we've been waiting for a long time. Yet "there is a time for everything, and a season for every activity under heaven" (Eccles. 3:1). God's timing is often very different from ours. One of the biggest mistakes we make is trying to rush God. We may think we are ready, but only God knows the perfect time. When the season's right, be assured that He will release you to do the things that are burning inside your heart.

Big Sister: *Loretta Fenton*

The first time I ever felt God speaking directly to me was through the Bible. I was 14 years old and had not been a Christian for very long—a matter of months. I attended a youth event where some young Christians from America were in the U.K. singing, dancing and performing drama sketches in schools and talking about their faith. The group made such an impact on me that I remember praying, *God, this is so what I want to do with my life. If I could use my love for singing and dancing and tell others about You at the same time, that would be my dream come true.*

I went home that night and prayed to God that one day He would give me my heart's desire. Then I opened my Bible, desperate to hear from God. To my amazement, the page it opened to spoke directly to me. It was Ecclesiastes 11:9 (*TEV*) and was titled "Advice to Young People." It said, "Young people, enjoy your youth. Be happy while you are still young. Do what you want to do, and follow your heart's desire. But remember that God is going to judge you for whatever you do." I was amazed. I couldn't believe that God was concerned enough with me and my dreams to tell me—all but outright—to go for it!

I held on to that promise from God, delighted that He had shown me that what He puts in our hearts as dreams is often an indication of what we are called to. That He wants us to be happy and fulfilled came as such a wonderful revelation to me. He wants to give us our heart's desires. This can really help you as a young person if you are beginning to think about what you want to do with your life.

I never forgot that verse. But it wasn't until five years later that I started to see the fruit of this promise. God amazingly sorted it out for me to attend the School of Creative Ministries. I then joined the World Wide Message Tribe and from there I was a part of Shine, a pop and R & B girl band. I have learned through all of this that God is faithful to His Word, and His Word is powerful and true.

WHAT DO I DO IN THE MEANTIME?

Look at the story of Joseph (see Gen. 37–41). He had a dream that God would use him massively. He was so excited that he couldn't keep his dream to himself. Unwisely, he told his older brothers that he would rule over them one day. Then, not surprisingly, his boasting got him thrown into a hole and sold into slavery. After many miserable years of struggling and suffering, his dream finally came to pass. A lesson we must learn from the life of Joseph is to be humble and wait patiently.

I have one friend who used to work in a Christian recording studio, serving teas. Now she is a well-known musician. She faithfully served God in the small things for years before she finally got to do the thing she'd dreamed about. I didn't even know she could sing—she kept it so quiet!

If you feel God has given you something to do in the future, hold on to it and store it up in your heart. Many young girls come up to me and reel off the news that they are going to be the next big thing in the Christian scene. Whatever dreams you have, keep them between you and God and continue praying and being faithful in the little things—serving at church, helping with the kids' ministry, putting the chairs away, and so on. These actions are ways of serving God and showing Him that you are willing to wait patiently.

However, what do we do when exciting opportunities and open doors come our way and we've got big decisions to make? Go to college or find a job? Do full-time church ministry or full-time work in the city? What about our dreams? When it comes to making these decisions, we can be certain that if we continue to seek God, He will continue to guide us. If we ask for wisdom, He will give it:

Many are the plans in a man's heart, but it is the LORD's purpose that prevails (Prov. 19:21).

In his heart a man plans his course, but the LORD determines his steps (Prov. 16:9).

Trust in the LORD with all your heart and lean not on your own understanding; in all your ways acknowledge him, and he will make your paths straight (Prov. 3:5).

Commit to the LORD whatever you do, and your plans will succeed (Prov. 16:3).

Big Sister: *Wendy Virgo*

I was taught from an early age that the Bible is very important. It not only tells us what God is like, the history of His people and how He wants us to live, but it also is a source of guidance to us. It helps us to make choices in our lives. Sometimes it speaks into our situation very specifically.

When I was 18, I went to college in London. I wanted to get a degree and be a teacher. In my final year, I needed a better sense of direction. Where did God want me to go next? I wanted to go abroad and tried applying to various places, but nothing opened up. An old friend got in touch and told me she had had a wonderful year with an overseas organization that placed students and young people in deprived countries to give voluntary aid. My friend had been working in a school in Malawi. This was what I wanted to do. It was adventurous and useful, and also was an opportunity to spread my wings and see another part of the world.

I obtained the necessary forms and began to fill them out. When I got to the bottom of the page, I realized I would need a reference. I thought my tutor would be a good person to ask, so I got up from the desk to find her. My hand was on the doorknob when a thought struck me, *She will ask me if I have prayed about this.* I knew the honest answer was no. I hesitated, *Perhaps I should pray first before seeing her.* So I went to my bed and prayed, *Lord, I am sorry I have assumed that this is okay with You without really seeking Your will. Please, will You speak to me now and help me to hear You clearly?* I opened my Bible. My eyes fell upon some verses in Psalm 32: "I will instruct you and teach you in the way you should go; I will counsel you and watch over you. Do not be like the horse or the mule, which have no understanding but must be controlled by bit and bridle or they will not come to you" (vv. 8-9). The words pierced my heart like an arrow. God was saying I must not rush ahead like an uncontrolled horse, doing what I thought was a good idea. I must wait patiently and trust Him to lead me. I stood up and stared at the form. Then slowly I tore it up.

Did I ever regret that decision? No. I am so glad God spoke into my life at that moment. A few weeks later, I began to date Terry, the man who became my husband and with whom I have had a very happy and fulfilling life as we have worked together for the kingdom of God.

IT'S IN HIS TIME

People are generally fascinated with finding out the future. Many go in search of answers by looking into astrology, palm reading, tarot cards and many other unreliable methods. However, apart from God, there's no one on this earth who can accurately predict our future. The Bible says that our times are in His hands (see Ps. 31:15). He knows what we will do with our lives—if we will marry and have children, what careers we will have and how long we'll live. He has our lives mapped out before us:

> All the days ordained for me were written in your book before one of them came to be (Ps. 139:16).

The unshakable truth is that there is no one else like you. God created you with gifts and abilities and a purpose to fulfill. What is that purpose and when will it be fulfilled? Only God knows, but as you continue to follow Him, He will teach you His ways and open the doors.

I remember being around the age of eight years old when my family took me to a Christian conference called the Downs Bible Week. I went to the children's meetings and stood on the chair singing along. Suddenly the words of a song gripped my little heart:

> I have a destiny I know I shall fulfill,
> I have a destiny in that city on a hill.
> I have a destiny and it's not an empty wish,
> For I know I was born for such a time as this.
>
> Long before the ages You predestined me
> To walk in all the works You have prepared for me.
> You've given me a part to play in history,
> By the power of Your Spirit working mightily.[1]

Being only eight years old, I didn't fully understand the words, but I did understand the basic sentiment. God had a plan for my life. I'd been "born for such a time as this," and for the first time in my life I knew I was here for a reason. It was so exciting! Home life was hard, and I slipped in and out of Christianity as I struggled with pain and heartache. When I returned to God and fully committed my life to him, I was 18. Ten years before that I had felt God give me a dream. Now, 10 years later, I finally had begun to walk in it.

You, too, have a destiny. It's not an empty wish that must live in a file named disappointment. God has planned for you to be alive today, and His hand is on your life. He is for you and He has works prepared in advance for you to do. It is only through Him that these things will come to pass. Don't allow yourself to believe you are a waste of space or a worthless dreamer. You have a destiny. Your life is for a reason. Hang on to Him and let His truth set you free. And don't ever stop dreaming big dreams for His kingdom and His glory. Amen!

CHAPTER 8

HOW TO HAVE A
QUIET TIME

In Psalm 119:9 (*NLT*), the writer asks the question, "How can a young person stay pure?" This is something we'd all love to know. How do we do this Christianity thing successfully? The problem seems to be the same for everyone: We love God and we want to follow Him, but it's hard to stay on track.

Every summer I attended a Christian family conference with my youth group. Together we experienced many deep things with God in a loving and supportive environment. One significant part of the conference was the Bible teaching, which was communicated in a simple and exciting way. I always returned home enthusiastic and fired up. By early September, once school started, my vows and good intentions slowly began to slip away as real life beckoned. I found it impossible to sustain my devotion without the support and presence of my summer experience. I didn't know where to start. I spiraled downward and each year by Christmas I was positively backslidden. This cycle continued until I grabbed the Bible with both hands and took hold of the answer to the psalmist's question myself:

By living according to your word (Ps. 119:9).

THE SPIRITUAL THIRST QUENCHER

Just as we drink water to stay alive, so living in God's Word enables us to survive in our world. Imagine a day without drinking any water. Most likely you would experience a bad headache and a very dry mouth. Now imagine a week. You simply could not survive. Our bodies are designed not to go even three days without water. Spiritually, many of us are dehydrated because we're not drinking enough. There are many ways to quench a spiritual thirst, and one way is through reading the Bible.

Over the years, I've found that the key to spiritual stability is living in God's Word. Each time I pick up the Bible and live my life according to it, I fall off the spiritual roller coaster and gain a sort of "God momentum." The Bible is crammed full of instruction, correction, wisdom, revelation and encouragement, which enables me to feed myself rather than just to rely on Christian events to keep me alive spiritually. These events then become a bonus rather than a lifeline.

> EACH TIME I PICK UP THE BIBLE AND LIVE MY LIFE ACCORDING TO IT, I FALL OFF THE SPIRITUAL ROLLER COASTER AND GAIN A SORT OF "GOD MOMENTUM."

All Scripture is God-breathed and is useful for teaching, rebuking, correcting and training in righteousness, so that the man [woman] of God may be thoroughly equipped for every good work (2 Tim. 3:16-17).

With renewed passion we need to pick up the Bible, but where exactly do we start? It isn't a novel, so it would be unwise to start at the beginning and expect to reach the end by next month! It is to be taken in stages—each of the 66 books it contains teaches us something different.

The Old Testament

The book of Genesis begins the story. It's the foundation of all we believe. Genesis 1–11 tells us that the eternal God created all things good. We were made in His image, for relationship and rulership over the earth. Yet in our freedom, we rebelled against Him, claiming to be our own god (the Fall). Then horrible things happened including murder (Cain and Abel), total corruption (except for Noah and his family in the flood) and pride reaching to heaven (the tower of Babel). If you look closely, Genesis includes some biology, astronomy, anthropology and chemistry!

But God's plan for us was never overturned. Starting with Abraham, He promised to bless a special family (the Jews) and through them bless the whole world. This set the stage for Jesus' birth almost 2,000 years later.

From Exodus to 2 Chronicles (look at the contents page of your Bible), the story line reveals God delivering His people from slavery in Egypt, giving them His Word (the Law) and His worship (the Tabernacle and later the Temple), and taking them to His special land (the Promised Land). Along the way bad things happened, but God was faithful in preparing for the final salvation in Jesus Christ.

In the middle of the Old Testament, there is a book called the Psalms—the prayer book of the Bible. It is a great thing to read a psalm each day. Here we learn how to pray, meditate, worship and be honest with God. Both individuals and groups used the psalms as prayers for private devotions and public praise, and we can do the same today.

After Psalms comes the book of Proverbs—a brilliant book full of short and snappy bits of wisdom from a king named

Solomon. Here's an example: "A fool's mouth is his undoing, and his lips are a snare to his soul" (Prov. 18:7). This is a great verse to pull us up when we've been gossiping or saying too much!

The final big section of the Old Testament is the prophets. These people are God's mouthpieces. They speak His words of love and warning into our lives and predict much of the future fulfilled in Jesus. Read Isaiah 53 for a heavy prophecy about His death for us.

The New Testament

The New Testament begins with the four Gospels: Matthew, Mark, Luke and John. They are "portraits" of Jesus rather than "photographs." Each writer selects his own special perspective on our Lord's birth, ministry, death and resurrection. They are either eyewitnesses to the events they record or eyewitnesses' immediate friends who did their homework before writing (see Luke 1:1-4). The Gospels are particularly amazing because they capture the words and actions of Jesus as He actually lived, and they climax with His death on the cross and His resurrection from the dead. In each Gospel, He is shown to be the eternal Son of God who became fully human like us, going through all we go through yet never blowing it—sinning:

> For we do not have a high priest who is unable to sympathize with our weaknesses, but we have one who has been tempted in every way, just as we are—yet was without sin (Heb. 4:15).

The book of Acts shows us how Jesus' mission was passed on to His disciples, how the Church grew and how what the Holy Spirit did through Jesus He continued to do through these men and women. This builds us up to believe that He can do the same things through us today.

Most of the rest of the New Testament contains letters. Paul—who gave up persecuting Christians and spent the rest of his life winning people to Jesus, experiencing God's power and starting churches—wrote 13 of them. Other apostles like James, Peter and John also wrote letters. These are windows into the Early Church. They are sharpening and vibrant encouragements, which are relevant and radical today.

We see that these Christians struggled with the same problems we have today, and we find that Jesus is the answer to every question (see Philippians). For deep teaching on the gospel, read Romans and Galatians (salvation isn't what we do, it is what Jesus has done—what He's made real by His Spirit and our family life together). For a simple study of the Christian life, read 1 John (about holy love). For practical wisdom on how to live, read James. To learn how Jesus fulfills the Old Testament priesthood and sacrificial system, read Hebrews. To be ready for Jesus' return, read 1 and 2 Thessalonians.

The last book of the Bible, Revelation, contains heavy visions of the conflict between God and the devil. While the battle rages on the earth, the saints sing in heaven. The outcome is sure: Jesus reigns and brings in a whole new order—the final judgment and restoration of the universe to God's great plan and purpose.

A Good Starting Place

Throughout the Bible the themes are the same, yet we're carried through a roller coaster of experiences and images of God the Creator, Redeemer, Father and Friend.

Where should you start? You could read a psalm and pray it in your own words. Or you could read a chapter in the Gospels and ask Jesus to help you know Him better. Think over what He says and does, and thank Him for what you see and learn. Ask Him to make you more like Himself.

You also can read passages and books of the Bible for help with your own problems. For example, James and Proverbs have good stuff on gossiping. Romans 8 tells us how to live a new life in the Spirit. Additionally, you can look up a single word in a Bible concordance and find all the places where it is used. The word "hope," for instance, will give you a lot of verses on what to look forward to. "Faith" will build you up for the present. "Love" will put you in the center of God's heart. The *Life Application Study Bible* (Zondervan Publishing House, 1991) is a big help in understanding what the message of the Bible is all about in everyday language. Get a modern translation like the *New International Version* or *New Living Translation*.

A TIME AND PLACE

We all live busy lives, but it really is possible for quiet times to become a simple and natural part of your everyday routine—it may just take a bit of discipline! The first thing is to be realistic about how much time you can set aside each day. This will determine whether you read a verse, a paragraph, a chapter or an entire book. If you set aside time each day, it will make a real difference in your growth and also in the way you react to the situations you face daily.

I know that when I regularly spend time with God and in the Bible, it totally transforms my reactions to things. Take today, for example: We just moved into a different house and decided to employ a tree surgeon to cut down some trees in order to get a bit more sunshine into our garden. Right in the middle of the tree cutting, my new next-door neighbor came around. She was not very happy and started to give specific instructions as to what we could and couldn't do with our trees. This was slightly annoying since we had gone through all the proper channels and were cutting the trees in compliance with council rules. I couldn't believe someone would get that upset about some greenery, but she really was devastated that her view of our house had been affected.

Unfortunately, Matt (the diplomat in the Redman family) was away, so I had to deal with Mrs. Moaner alone. To my surprise, I initially managed to stay calm and be polite while ushering her off the premises. But once I got indoors, I became more and more enraged! In fact, by the time I spoke to Matt, I was furious. I decided that the next time I saw her I would say something really rude and horrible and tell her just what I thought of her. I looked out of the window at her house and hoped for a rematch soon. Then I picked up my Bible and decided to have a quiet time before work. I turned to the book of Proverbs and my mouth dropped open as I read:

> With his mouth the godless destroys his neighbor, but through knowledge the righteous escape (Prov. 11:9).

> A man who lacks judgment derides his neighbor, but a man of understanding holds his tongue (Prov. 11:12).

In some people's eyes, I had every right to tear her to shreds for her rudeness, but not in God's eyes. Wisdom and godliness say to hold your tongue. Imagine if I had retaliated! To fall into a dispute with our neighbors in the first few months of living here would not be wise or appropriate—first, because we are Christians, and second, because we hope to live here for some time. I sighed and thanked God for His wonderful wisdom and His gentle rebuke. I love the way God speaks to me so directly through the Bible in my everyday, ordinary life.

There is no such thing as the perfect time or place for a quiet time, but God can speak to us powerfully and specifically anywhere and anytime. Only we know what suits each of us best. I am a bit of a morning person, so it works best for me to grab some time before breakfast while everyone else is sleeping. When I lived in a house with four other girls, there was never a quiet moment, so we used to put up a Do Not Disturb sign on the door or sneak into the bathroom if we were having a quiet time and did not want to be interrupted. (By the way, God is not legalistic and will not love you any less if things are crazy and you don't manage to squeeze in a quiet time. Please don't forget grace!)

Quiet times don't have to start at 4 A.M. or last for one hour. They are much simpler than that. Just like eating breakfast or applying makeup, they can become a quick and easy but essential part of our day.

QUIET-TIME SUGGESTIONS

To finish this chapter, I've put together three different types of quiet times. The best one for you depends on how much time you have. Each section includes a simple framework that is easy to follow and some study notes and books should you want to go a bit deeper. I hope they help.

Small (5 minutes)

Start: Read a verse such as Proverbs 16:28: "A gossip separates close friends," or Psalm 139:23-24: "Search me, O God, and know my heart; test me and know my anxious thoughts. See if there is any offensive way in me, and lead me in the way everlasting."

Stop: Now pray through the verse. What does it mean to you? Have you gossiped or been gossiped about? What do you want to say to God about it? Is there anything on your heart that you are worried about, or is there something bugging you that you need to say you're sorry for or to tell God about? Talk to Him now.

Wait: Just because you only have time for a small quiet time today doesn't mean it has to be a one-way conversation. You still have time to listen, so spend a few minutes waiting to hear God. It is a good idea to keep a pen and paper handy, so you can write down any thoughts or verses that come to mind. Even if you've waited and not heard anything specific, ask Him to give you peace and strength for today.

Other good bits to read during a small quiet time are verses from Ephesians, Philippians, Matthew, Mark, Luke, John, 1 John and Jude.

Helpful Resources
Book: *Piercing Proverbs* by Melody Carlson (Multnomah Publishers, 2002).

Medium (10-15 minutes)
Start: Because you've got a bit more time, why not try reading a couple of paragraphs from somewhere like Titus 2? Here is a little section from *THE MESSAGE*:

> We're being shown how to turn our backs on a godless, indulgent life, and how to take on a God-filled, God-honoring life. This new life is starting right now, and is whetting our appetites for the glorious day when our great God and Savior, Jesus Christ, appears. He offered himself as a sacrifice to free us from a dark, rebellious life into this good, pure life, making us a people he can be proud of, energetic in goodness (vv. 12-14).

Stop: This passage reveals that God is changing us from being people who are consumed with sin to people who are full of Him. Read through the verses again. What areas in your life has

God changed for the better? What areas do you think still need to be addressed in order for you to honor God? Write a list of anything that comes to mind.

Wait: Now look over your list. Thank God for the things He has done in your life already. It is always good to stop and recognize the hand of God on your life. Next spend some time praying and commit to Him the things that you still struggle with, and then ask Him to help you.

Other good bits to read during a medium quiet time are verses from Colossians, Hebrews, Genesis 1–11, Daniel, Ruth, Esther, 1 Timothy and 2 Timothy.

Helpful Resources
Book: *The Site: Daily Hits on God's Word* compiled by Craig Borlase (Hodder and Stoughton, 2000).
Study guide: *First Timothy and Titus: Fighting the Good Fight* by John Stott (Intervarsity Press, 1998).

Large (15-30 minutes)
Start: You have heaps of time, so why not try reading a chapter from Romans? Here's an excerpt from Romans 2:12-13 (*THE MESSAGE*):

> If you sin without knowing what you're doing, God takes that into account. But if you sin knowing full well what you're doing, that's a different story entirely. Merely hearing God's law is a waste of your time if you don't do what he commands. Doing, not hearing, is what makes the difference with God.

Stop: Why not find a study guide for the book of Romans and see if you can get a better insight into what Paul is writing?

Through learning, you can reach a deeper level of understanding God's laws and God's character.

Wait: Have you been hearing but not doing? Spend some time being quiet and see if you hear an answer. Finish by praying through the things this passage has shown you about God and about your own life, and then just worship Him for a while. Play a CD that will help you to concentrate and meet with God.

Other good bits to read during a large quiet time are chapters from Acts, Galatians, Isaiah, 1 Corinthians, 2 Corinthians, 1 Samuel, 2 Samuel and Revelation.

Helpful Resources

Book: *You've Got Mail* by Stephen Travis (Authentic Media, 2002).
Study guide: *Cover to Cover* by Selwyn Hughes and Trevor Partridge (Broadman and Holman Publishers, 1999).

WHERE I FOUND HELP

Advice from Your Soul Sisters

This section features inspiring and wise words from big sisters around the globe. I pray it will spur you on to pick up the big Book and find God's wisdom for yourself.

ANNIE FLACK

Don't let anyone look down on you because you are young, but set an example for the believers in speech, in life, in love, in faith and in purity (1 Tim. 4:12).

When I became a Christian at the age of 14, this was one of the first Bible verses I read. I loved the idea of not letting anyone look down on me because of my age. It was quite a while later before I paid much attention to the second half of the verse and realized I actually had a responsibility. Instead of walking around knowing I was just as good as any of the Christian oldies, I actually was called to live as an example to them. I was humbled and encouraged that God wanted my life to be an example for others: "Set an example for the believers in speech, in life, in love, in faith and in purity." I love the fact that God doesn't wait for us to grow old before He asks anything of us. He wants to use our lives to impact His kingdom, no matter how old or young we are.

LOU FELLINGHAM

Therefore, since we have a great high priest who has gone through the heavens, Jesus the Son of God, let us hold firmly to the faith we profess. For we do not have a high priest who is unable to sympathize with our weaknesses, but we have one who has been tempted in every way, just as we are—yet was without sin. Let us then approach the throne of grace with confidence, so that we may receive mercy and find grace to help us in our time of need (Heb. 4:14-16).

This Scripture has helped me tremendously, because it has made me realize that I don't have to have everything sorted out before I come to God. Sometimes I've felt that I can't speak to God, or He won't understand, or I have to spend a certain number of hours reading my Bible before I can enter His presence. But that's not what the Bible says! It doesn't say that once I've got everything figured out then I can come to Him. It says that as I come to Him, I receive mercy and grace to help me in my time of need.

SHELLEY GIGLIO

So do not fear, for I am with you; do not be dismayed, for I am your God. I will strengthen you and help you; I will uphold you with my righteous right hand (Isa. 41:10).

One of the verses that has meant the most to me I learned back when I was quite young. I was 13 years old and attended a school that enrolled students with great diversity in their backgrounds.

I was quite intimidated by the school's size and the confronting nature of most of the students. One time, several of the students bullied me because they believed I had been involved in something that I had not been part of. I was terrified. At the age of 13, I learned a priceless lesson about the faithfulness of God. I memorized Isaiah 41:10 and quoted it to myself for days as the taunting continued. I was not harmed, I overcame and I learned that day to lean on the Word of God for encouragement, comfort and support in times of great need. The truth truly set me free. And I still need it as desperately today as I did then!

DARLENE ZSCHECH

You shaped me first inside, then out; you formed me in my mother's womb. I thank you, High God—you're breathtaking! Body and soul, I am marvelously made! I worship in adoration—what a creation! (Ps. 139:13-14, *THE MESSAGE*).

I became a Christian when I was 15 years old. My family had split, and somehow I found myself taking on a lot of the blame and a tremendous amount of guilt. My formative years had become my worst nightmare—not the picture-perfect home and family I'd always dreamed of. Then I met Jesus.

His Word, His promise and His overwhelming love started to redefine in my heart who I was, and most important, *whose I was*. Through spending time reading the Bible, I noticed God starting to heal my heart and making me new. My life is truly miraculous, and I can confidently say that He's turned my mourning into dancing.

The Scripture that spoke so clearly into the core of me at that time was Psalm 139. It beautifully tells that God knew me inside and out before I was born and that He made me wonderfully complex to bring Him glory all the days of my life. It also says that every single day of my life was recorded in His book (v. 16). (I would *so* love to see that book!) And in verse 24 (*NLT*) it says, "Point out anything in me that offends you, and lead me along the path of everlasting life."

There you have it—my focus from those days to today is that I love my God with all I am, and He will always find me ready to worship and obey. May I be known as someone who loves her Lord and lifts the lives of people. I discovered that when you allow God to transform your heart and life as a young person, your life will flourish in ways that you never even dared to dream about.

KARA TOWNSEND

Love is patient, love is kind. It does not envy, it does not boast, it is not proud. It is not rude, it is not self-seeking, it is not easily angered, it keeps no record of wrongs. Love does not delight in evil but rejoices with the truth. It always protects, always trusts, always hopes, always perseveres (1 Cor. 13:4-7).

When I was 12 years old, I sat on my bed and suddenly realized that I wanted to get to know God for myself. I started reading my Bible in Genesis, but quickly lost interest. As I stumbled upon this well-known passage, I actually *felt* for the first time in my life that I wanted to be like Jesus. I decided to break down the qualities of love and try to follow them in my life. I made a chart with a different "personality" of love to work on each day (e.g., patience, then kindness). I began to see God soften my heart toward my brothers, my parents and my annoying class-mates as I tried to apply His Word to my life. I didn't have a clue what I was doing, but I had to start somewhere. Somehow, though, God used it to bring to mind the qualities He is still growing in me today.

CHRISTY WIMBER

I came to you in weakness and fear, and with much trembling. My message and my preaching were not with wise and persuasive words, but with a demonstration of the Spirit's power, so that your faith might not rest on men's wisdom, but on God's power (1 Cor. 2:3-5).

A few years ago, I started putting together worship events around the world. I always used to make other people get on stage and do the "up front" stuff. I preferred to lead behind-the-scenes where it felt safer. When my father-in-law started telling me I needed to get out there and speak to the people, my first response was, "No way!" Because I always had been around so many gifted people, I really thought that what I had to offer would never be as good or as neatly polished. However, I did start speaking and ministering, and slowly over the years it has become easier.

> IT DOESN'T MATTER HOW STUPID OR WEAK I FEEL. WHAT MATTERS IS THAT I DO WHAT GOD ASKS OF ME AND THAT I KEEP LOOKING TO HIM.

I remember one occasion when I led a ministry time in front of a few thousand people; I was literally shaking. The Lord showed me the above verse and reassured me that all I needed to do was show up and look for what He was doing.

It doesn't matter how stupid or weak I feel. What matters is that I do what God asks of me and that I keep looking to Him. So often we put too much pressure on ourselves and what we have to offer. I believe that the weaker I feel, the better it can be—less of me and more of Jesus.

ANDY ARGANDA

Come to me, all you who are weary and burdened, and I will give you rest. Take my yoke upon you and learn from me, for I am gentle and humble in heart, and you will find rest for your souls. For my yoke is easy and my burden is light (Matt. 11:28-30).

This Scripture has always been a great source of hope and comfort to me. There have been a number of times in my life where loved ones around me suffered terrible illnesses. My youngest sister was diagnosed with leukemia when she was two-and-a-half years old (she is now 19 and completely healthy). My brother died of a chromosome disease. A very dear friend of mine died of cancer a couple of years ago, and most recently my other sister was diagnosed with multiple sclerosis.

During each of these scary times of wondering what the diagnosis and outcome were going to be, I was reminded of this great Scripture. As I poured my heart out to Jesus, He was faithful in carrying my burden, and I managed to find peace of mind and rest in Him. The Bible never ceases to amaze me. Daily I come across new truths and promises written years and years ago yet still so valid and true for what is happening in my life today.

ALI MACINNES

My grace is sufficient for you, for my power is made perfect in weakness (2 Cor. 12:9).

For it is by grace you have been saved, through faith—and this not from yourselves, it is the gift of God—not by works, so that no one can boast (Eph. 2:8-9).

A few years ago, I went through a time of depression. Not "having a bad day" depressed but months of pain leading up to medication and counseling, and a few suicidal thoughts along the way. I had nothing to look forward to. Over a period of time I lost all confidence, couldn't cope with normal life, felt frightened in crowds and lost all sense of having hope and a future. It was a really horrible period of tears and emptiness, and at the time I couldn't imagine things would ever be any different.

During this time, I found it really hard to read my Bible and pray. I chatted with a couple of wise friends who'd experienced the whole depression thing. They told me it was common and that I needed to remember there are times in life when it's okay simply to rest in God's presence. It was a hard lesson to learn. On the one hand, I felt guilty for not reading my Bible, and on the other, I just knew I couldn't. I was lethargic and couldn't really concentrate on anything, so I had to give in. In the end, the lesson I learned was this: The Father's love for me is not, and will never be, based on what I have or have not done—past, present or future. God wasn't yelling at me in my depressed state, "Why aren't you reading your Bible? How dare you? Get on with life and stop moping about!" Instead, He quieted me with His love, speaking to me gently and tenderly.

And Jesus did heal me. He began a process that is still going on today. As I look back on that time of depression, I can't pretend it wasn't horrible, but neither can I bring myself to regret it. It was a refining time—a time to clear out some of the mess that had built up over the years. God used that painful season to show me who I am in Him, what I'm called to and that my life and security only come from being firmly rooted in Him.

DIANE LOUISE JORDAN

And a voice from heaven said, "This is my Son, whom I love; with him I am well pleased" (Matt. 3:17).

I love this Scripture because it really helps me to understand how much God loves me. Jesus has just been baptized, and up until this point, all we know is that He is a carpenter. His ministry hasn't even begun, yet God says that He *loves* Jesus and He is well pleased with His Son. This is exactly how God loves us! He loves us and is well pleased with us simply because we're His sons and daughters—not because of our efforts. Over the years, this Scripture has encouraged me to realize that our perfect Father (who doesn't make mistakes) designed each of us to be uniquely as we are. And if we're good enough for God, we must be good enough for the world.

CARRIE GRANT

She gets up while it is still dark; she provides food for her family and portions for her servant girls. She considers a field and buys it; out of her earnings she plants a vineyard (Prov. 31:15-16).

I love these verses because they are so empowering for women today. Sometimes people think that to be a totally satisfied Christian woman all you do is sit at home all day in unfashionable clothes, praying for a husband and then bearing him some children. There's nothing wrong with this, but the woman in Proverbs is a woman who provides for and takes care of her family and staff—and is a property developer, too! Now, for me, that's inspiring and totally cool!

DEBBY WRIGHT

Love the Lord your God with all your heart and . . . love your neighbor as yourself (Luke 10:27).

I have a tendency to become overly introspective and self-absorbed, and the best antidote to that stuff in my life is to start living by these two commandments. There simply is nothing more fun and wonderful than being free to worship God. It completely lifts me out of my introspection and places me firmly before the throne of God. When I think of others and try to serve them, I begin to feel relationally healthy and full of purpose. Putting these two commandments into practice practically settles who I am and what I am for. It's no wonder Jesus said that all the Law and the prophets hang on these two commandments.

CINDY REITHMEIR

In all their distress he too was distressed, and the angel of his presence saved them. In his love and mercy he redeemed them; he lifted them up and carried them all the days of old (Isa. 63:9).

I came across this Scripture in the middle of a family crisis. I could not see any way around or past the situation. I was in constant turmoil over the thought of my family being torn apart and our relationships being damaged beyond repair. I was beginning to understand that I was not in control and the only way we could survive was if God rescued us.

I was grateful when I read this verse because it reminded me that God felt my fear and anguish as deeply as I felt them. He was ready to come to me in love, mercy and redemption; and He was willing and able to lift me up and carry me through each day. My one and only assurance in life is Jesus, and this was one of the times when I was reminded of what a great gift His presence is in times of difficulty.

RACHEL FELLINGHAM

Don't let anyone look down on you because you are young, but set an example for the believers in speech, in life, in love, in faith and in purity (1 Tim. 4:12).

When I was 15, this verse in 1 Timothy really encouraged me. Quite often people think you have to be experienced or ancient for God to be able to use you. I wanted to be able to do things for God, but people don't always take you seriously when you are young. This verse says that God can use you as a young person to be an example—even to older people. It really helped me go for it and not worry about what others thought of me.

SARAH HUNTER

Now faith is being sure of what we hope for and certain of what we do not see (Heb. 11:1).

Faith in God doesn't change when things get difficult. As this verse tells us, faith is the conviction of things not seen. I have faith in who God is. I have faith in His goodness and kindness, His justice and His love. I have faith that though things may get worse, He will never change.

I grew up in a Christian family, but from the age of 2 until I was 13, I was abused at home by my stepdad. I never told anyone about the abuse, but I eventually found a way to move in with my father and his wife. At first things went pretty well, but my dad became addicted to alcohol and prescription drugs. When I was 18, two days before Christmas, I received a phone call telling me my dad had choked and slipped into a coma. Two days later, on Christmas, he died.

Where is God when we suffer? The answer is that He is as close to us in the dark valleys as He is when we're on top of the world. Suffering isn't what draws us away from God. In many ways, it is what draws us closer. When we

> GOD IS AS CLOSE TO US IN THE DARK VALLEYS AS HE IS WHEN WE'RE ON TOP OF THE WORLD.

suffer, we're forced to remove all of our faith in the "good life" we see around us and instead place our faith and hope in God alone.

KATE VIRGO

Delight yourself in the LORD and he will give you the desires of your heart (Ps. 37:4).

I grew up in a Christian family, which I appreciated and enjoyed until I was about 17. I then felt as though a lot of decisions had been made for me, and I wondered if I was only a Christian because of my upbringing. I became convinced Christianity was just a bunch of rules I had to follow, which were meant to stop me from having fun. I panicked and rebelled against my parents and the Church in order to search for what I thought was the real meaning of life. I ended up traveling around Australia—which I loved—but all I really was doing was putting off decisions about my future.

Upon returning to England, I was restless, unhappy and felt very uncertain about the future. That Christmas my parents asked me to go to church with them. I went feeling very cynical, but it actually wasn't too bad. A lady there spoke about God's love and how it was unconditional. Over the next few months, I started a journey of actually getting to know God and realizing the truth that we are happiest when we are in God's will. He knows what is best for us, and He knows that we are truly fulfilled when we are walking close to Him. God doesn't watch over us, waiting for us to make our next mistake; instead, He lovingly guides us and offers forgiveness when we blow it.

ANNIE FLACK

Let us then approach the throne of grace with confidence, so that we may receive mercy and find grace to help us in our time of need (Heb. 4:16).

So often in life I find myself shying away from God's presence. When I know I've not been living the way He asks me to or when I haven't spent time with Him for a while, instead of running to Him, I try and hide away. This verse has reminded me many times that drawing close to God isn't about coming to get a well-deserved smack! When we move toward His throne, we find grace, love and mercy. When I remember this, I'm much quicker to turn myself around and draw near to Him. When I was 15, some friends and I turned this verse into a little song so that we could remember it. The song wasn't very good, but it's been amazing how many times the song has come to mind just at the right times—reminding me to come confidently into His presence, knowing that I'll always be met with grace and mercy.

RENSKE AERTS

For as the heavens are high above the earth, so great is His mercy toward those who fear Him; as far as the east is from the west, so far has He removed our transgressions from us (Ps. 103:11-12, *NKJV*).

As a young teenager, I struggled with feelings of guilt. I guess I was a bit of a rebel. I didn't want to conform to the "rules" of Christianity, and I lived on the edge, sometimes falling off the wrong side. I'd experienced from some people a cold and merciless faith. But there was a radical turn in my spiritual life when God revealed to me through the Bible that His mercy is without end. "As far as the east is from the west"—that's even far enough for me!

ALI MacINNES

Being confident of this, that he who began a good work in you will carry it on to completion until the day of Christ Jesus (Phil. 1:6).

I love to come back to this verse time and time again—particularly when I'm struggling with the same old sin in my life, or when I feel weighed down by hurts that I so desperately long to be free from. This verse is God's promise to me that He will not give up on me. He won't abandon me, get tired of me or stop forgiving me, but He *will* carry on the good work He started. It is God, not me, who changes me to make me more like His Son.

I hope and pray that God's Word will truly be a lamp to your
feet as you live a life of worship before Him. Go for it!
Much love,
Beth

ENDNOTES

Chapter 1

1. Mary Pytches, *Who Am I?: Discovering Your Identity in Christ* (London: Hodder and Stoughton, 1999), pp. 78-79.
2. Ibid., p. 146.

Chapter 3

1. Rebecca St. James, *Wait for Me* (Nashville, TN: Thomas Nelson, 2002), p. 7.
2. Source unknown.

Chapter 6

1. Judy Pruett, "The Grace of God," copyright 1990. All rights reserved. Used by permission.

Chapter 7

1. Mark Altrogge, "I Have a Destiny," © 1986 PDI Praise/BMI (adm. by Integrity's Praise! Music) c/o Integrity Media, Inc., 1000 Cody Road, Mobile, AL 36695

More Breakthrough Books from Soul Survivor

The Unquenchable Worshipper
Coming Back to the
Heart of Worship
Matt Redman
Gift Hardcover • 128 pages
ISBN 08307.29135

The Heart of Worship Files
Featuring Contributions by Some
of Today's Most Experienced
Lead Worshippers
Compiled by Matt Redman
Gift Hardcover • 208 pages
ISBN 08307.32616

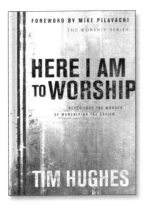

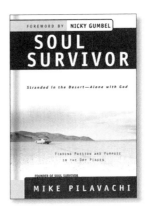

Here I Am to Worship
Never Lose the Wonder of
Worshiping the Savior
Tim Hughes
Gift Hardcover • 128 pages
ISBN 08307.33221
Available March 2004

Soul Survivor
Finding Passion and Purpose
in the Dry Places
Mike Pilavachi
Trade Paper • 120 pages
ISBN 08307.33248

RADICALLY NEW WAY TO REACH YOUNG PEOPLE

soulsurvivor

If you want to inspire and equip young people, **Soul Survivor En-counter** is the key. Originating in England, Soul Survivor has released young leaders for Christ by teaching them about worship, action evangelism and social justice.

With **Soul Survivor Encounter**, you can use the successful elements of the Soul Survivor ministry to create in your young people a passionate commitment to worshiping God and putting their faith into action.

This biblical and relevant program is sure to ignite a revolution in youth ministry that will impact generations to come. Be a part of it!

Soul Survivor Kit
5 *Real Life & Living Out Loud Student Magazines*, 1 *Real Life & Living Out Loud Leader's Guide*, 1 *Real Life & Living Out Loud DVD*, *The Soul Survivor Guide to Youth Ministry*, *Soul Survivor Prayer Ministry*, and *Soul Survivor Guide to Service Projects.*
ISBN 08307.35267

Real Life & Living Out Loud Student Magazine
ISBN 08307.35364

Real Life & Living Out Loud Leader's Guide
ISBN 08307.35313

Real Life & Living Out Loud DVD
UPC 607135.008927

The Soul Survivor Guide to Youth Ministry
ISBN 08307.35305

Soul Survivor Prayer Ministry
ISBN 08307.35275

Soul Survivor Guide to Service Projects
ISBN 08307.35291

Soul Survivor Encounter is available at your local Christian bookstore, or by calling 1-800-4-GOSPEL.

www.SoulSurvivorEncounter.com

Gospel Light